SAGGISTICA 8

ESSAYS ON
ITALIAN AMERICAN LITERATURE AND CULTURE

ESSAYS ON
ITALIAN AMERICAN LITERATURE AND CULTURE

edited by

DENNIS BARONE

and

PETER COVINO

BORDIGHERA PRESS

Library of Congress Control Number: 2012936723

Cover art: Untitled, New York City/Rome by Liana Miuccio www.lianaphoto.com
Copyright 2011 remains exclusive property of the photographer.

The photograph is part of a multimedia exhibit titled "Double Vision/Doppia Visione," by Italian and USA photographer Liana Miuccio featuring photos and videos from her bi-cultural identity. The portraits of her family in the US and Italy, and the dual urban landscapes of New York and Rome, go beyond depicting Miuccio's memories and succeed in telling the story of many who live with two cultures.

Printed in the United States.

Published by
BORDIGHERA PRESS
John D. Calandra Italian American Institute
25 W. 43rd Street, 17th Floor
New York, NY 10036

SAGGISTICA 8
ISBN 978-1-59954-035-1

Contents

PETER COVINO

INTRODUCTION

The year 2010 represents a watershed in Italian American literature and related literary and critical writing. The field has gone from a fledgling and sometimes idiosyncratic body of work difficult to classify, to a fully realized and vibrant community of scholars with an ever-growing transnational readership that continues to attract attention from mainstream presses, and larger economic and political communities as well. Thanks to considerable innovations with the Internet and in related digital media, "Italian American characters" have searched and found *many* authors and a fully engaged critical reception, in a postmodern and post-Pirandellian age. With the Modern Language Association sponsored publication of Edvige Giunta's and Kathleen Zamboni McCormick's *Teaching Italian American Literature, Film, and Popular Culture* and the soon-to-be translated second volume of *Italoamericana,* Francesco Durante's tomes that chronicle the history of Italian literary production from the early colonial period to World War II, these important conversations that foreground the growing scholarship about Italian American literature and culture have already begun to multiply exponentially.

Those recent contributions to the field have been augmented by a second and now third generation of scholars led by the groundbreaking work of Richard Gambino, Rose Basile Green, and other notable more recent scholarship by Fred Gardaphè, Anthony Tamburri, Mary Jo Bona, Robert Viscusi, Josephine Guttoso Hendin, Pellegrino D'Acierno, and others too numerous to mention here. Gardaphè, Tamburri, Bona, Hendin, and Giunta have also been instrumental in nurturing the growth of the widely influential Italian American Discussion Group of the Modern Language Association, which continues to set the academic course for the discussion and production of crucial Italian American literary and cultural texts. This current volume collects and expands on many of the ideas explored during the Discussion Group's ten-plus years of existence; all but one of the essays were presented, in some form or other, during the Modern Language Association annual conventions. Scholarly writing about

Italian American literature and culture has arguably entered its second fully and critically engaged decade of sustained conversation and inquiry—this collection of essays endeavors to highlight the vitality of these inquiries and offer suggestions for continuing research and enjoyment. Moreover, we have tried whenever possible, to present essays that can also appeal to a more general and widespread audience by minimizing potentially confusing theoretical jargon.

Many of the ideas explored in this collection were cross-pollinated and given additional encouragement during sessions of the American Italian Historical Association (AIHA) conferences and, in more recent years, the City University of New York Calandra Institute's Annual Spring Conference on issues relevant to Italian American Studies, among other recent gatherings. Additionally, Professor Pellegrino D'Acierno's recently convened four-day conference, *For a Dangerous Pedagogy: A Manifesto for Italian and Italian American Studies* (April 14–17, 2010), deserves special mention for its wide-ranging, irreverent, and provocative inclusiveness, as this gathering saw three disparate academic institutions—the Hofstra Cultural Center, Hofstra University; The Italian Academy for Advanced Studies in America, Columbia University; and the Casa Italiana Zerilli-Marimò, New York University—work to bring together some of the most important scholars of Italian American, Italian, and transnational literatures writing today. This necessary dialogue between Italian studies and Italian American studies (and other ethnic and transnational fields of inquiry), needs to continue to flourish in order to insure the viability of these fields, beyond reductive and/or nostalgic and sentimental iterations of an ethnic, Italian, and/or Italian American imaginary other. Indeed, we are grateful for the ever-expanding venues and professional platforms that are being utilized to expound these important cultural forays and exchanges. This collection of essays both encourages and demystifies some of the wide variety of studies in the field of Italian American literature and culture, with the specific goal of attracting and welcoming more scholars and all others interested in the lively and vibrant discourse of this growing ethno-cultural conversation.

As a consequence of America's ongoing economic ascendancy, for better or worse, Italian American literary production and criticism continues to be the standard bearer across a transnational context; even as Italianist discourses have given rise to growing numbers of volumes both creative and critical in countries throughout the Italian diaspora. From everywhere in North America, Central America, and South America, to Australia and New Zealand, critics are documenting the literary history and production of peoples of Italian heritage. Many of these countries, America, Canada, and Italy most notably, are also making crucial linkages to people of other ethnic and marginalized groups within their own countries and across national borders. The cultural conversation appears definitively to have outstripped limited capitalistic notions of import, export, and travel-related romanticizing; and Italian American culture is finally emerging from the shadows, or more aptly, the centuries-long inferiority complex, thrust upon it by Greek, Roman, and Italian Renaissance cultural production especially.

With the growing numbers of intellectuals in national and international cultural organizations comes the concomitant burden of preserving and further developing an inclusive and representative cultural patrimony. Italian American literature has entered a new phase of postcolonial sophistication—what scholar-critic Robert Viscusi calls "Global Italian America"—and scholars continue to educate a growing public about the dangers of earlier reductive and stereotypical discourses. Viscusi argues convincingly that "nationalist ideologies" and the "fetish of a standard language" are being dismantled and newly interrogated ("History" 56). Literary and cultural criticism help us to combat the stultifying, deeply rooted silence (*omertà*) endemic to our patriarchal heritage, and further elucidate the rich lessons of our many and divergent contemporary experiences.

This collection of essays is also presented as a specific invitation to continue the cultural conversation and explore more fully engaged alternative intellectual literary and cultural traditions. Since all of the essays were presented at conferences, you will note an appealing and accessible attention to orality and often an inviting conversational tone. The collection is likewise arranged with the intention of tracing a logical arc—both with regard to organizational expansion and to historically relevant trends—in the growing progression of the field of Italian American literature. Immediately following this introductory essay we include Gina Miele's incisive exploration and overview of the efficacy and growth of Italian American literature and culture in four academic institutions that offer varying degrees of specialization in the field. Miele also muses about the future of Italian American literature and the larger degree-granting possibilities for the field. Some of the essays included here explore fullfledged and/or half-hearted rejections of Italian American ethnicity. Joseph Conte, for example, explores the historical and socio-cultural reasons for actor Oscar De Corti's shifting identity from Italian to Native American. Roseanna Giannini Quinn argues persuasively for the lasting influence of the experimental prose stylist Carole Maso on other experimental writers, Italian Americans among them, by offering close readings of three of Maso's recent memoirs, all of which continue to challenge genre categorization between poetry and prose.

That innovative study of autobiographical Italian American feminist writing across the genres of novel writing, memoir, and essay writing is furthered by Kathleen Zamboni McCormick, who concentrates her remarks on the migration of Italian American women writers into an urban intellectual milieu, even as they preserve and update the possibilities of Italian American identity and cultural and professional achievement. Tracy Floreani traces the cultural negotiations of fictional Italian Americans living in the American South and analyzes the twist that Southern grotesque style adds to this narrative. Her essay speaks keenly to the regional influences of American culture on Italian American literature while also claiming space for an expanded understanding of ethnically inflected literature beyond the well-established East Coast urban hubs.

Two essays, each devoted to individual Italian American poets, Jim Cocola's on Vincent Ferrini and John Domini's on W.S. Di Piero, frame a broader discussion about the power of close reading and the value of deconstructing linguistic experience at the level of each sound, syllable, and even dialect phrase. In the case of Ferrini, Cocola offers an especially compelling theoretical argument for the lasting value of Ferrini's dialect poems rather than poems that may be more familiar to readers. Nancy Caronia provides fascinating insight into Bruce Springsteen's Italian American identity and the cultural import of a public figure's role as an intermediary during times of political crisis. Caronia links Springsteen to an oratorical tradition that includes Mario Cuomo and harkens back even to early Roman figures of political consciousness. Finally, Michael Antonucci weighs in as a respondent offering commentary and pointed highlights on the remarks of some of the fields best second- and third-generation scholars already mentioned, who at the tenth meeting of the Modern Language Association Italian American Discussion Group plenary, offered an overview of the past ten years and outlined next steps for a growing generation of Italian American, Italianist, and transnational scholars with a bolder vision for the continued development of the field.

After a dozen years, the MLA Discussion Group on Italian American Literature has substantial reason for celebration and pride. The sampling of essays collected here attests to the quality and the variety of its programs, as does the fact that many other Discussion Group presentations have been published in journals, in edited essay collections, and as monographs. Notwithstanding this considerable progress, Fred Gardaphè reminds us that the original proposals to form the Italian American Discussion Group had twice been rejected before acceptance. Clearly, the urgent need to persevere in our advocacy efforts on behalf of this expanding discipline cannot be underestimated. The interest in the field of Italian American studies remains substantial, and ever-welcoming to even bolder and more fully engaged scholarly and literary production.

Works Cited

Bona, Mary Jo. *Claiming a Tradition: Italian American Women Writers.* Carbondale, IL: Southern Illinois UP, 1999.

Durante, Francesco. *Italoamericana: storia e letteratura degli Italiani negli Stati Uniti 1880–1943.* Milano: Mondadori, 2005.

Gardaphè, Fred. *Italian Signs, American Streets: The Evolution of Italian American Narrative.* Durham, NC: Duke UP, 1996.

Giunta, Edvidge. *Writing With an Accent: Contemporary Italian American Women Authors.* New York: Palgrave, 2002.

___, and Kathleen Zamboni McCormick, eds. *Teaching Italian American Literature, Film and Popular Culture.* New York: MLA, 2010.

Green, Rose Basile. *The Italian-American Novel: A Document of the Interaction of Two Cultures.* Cranbury, NJ: Farleigh Dickinson UP, 1974.

Tamburri, Anthony Julian. *A Semiotic of Ethnicity: In (Re)cogition of the Italian/American Writer.* Albany, NY: State U of New York P, 1998.

Viscusi, Robert. *Buried Caesars and Other Secrets of Italian American Writing.* New York: SUNY P, 2006.

___. "The History of Italian American Liteary Studies." Giunta and Zamboni McCormick, eds.

GINA M. MIELE

DEVISING THE GLOBAL CLASSROOM
How Italian American Studies Can Break Forth from the Traditional Learning Community[1]

This essay represents the first stage of an ethnographical study of the role of Italian American academic and cultural institutes as centers of public intellectual inquiry and discourse. Using four Italian American centers in the New York metropolitan area as models (The John D. Calandra Italian American Institute, Queens College; The Joseph and Elda Coccia Institute for the Italian Experience in America, Montclair State University; The Hostra Cultural Center's Italian American Experience Lecture Series, Hofstra University; and the Center for Italian Studies, Stony Brook University), I examine public-minded educational practices and empirical methodologies, and consider how cultural institutes teach and support literature, history, and culture outside of the classroom. My conversations with the directors and scholars affiliated with each institute focused on the challenges encountered when academics bring Italian American literature to the community, the expected outcomes, the intended learner and what he or she brings to the learning process, and how personal and communal experience and memory intersect with the analysis of a literary text.

The objective of this continuing study is to document the challenges of undertaking a constructivist teaching approach from the perspectives of both institute personnel and intended learners. I provide accounts of how the missions and everyday practices of institute directors, scholars,

[1] A companion version of this article can be consulted in: "Modern Agoras: A Comparativist Study of Public Teaching at Italian American Institutes," *The Harvard College Journal of Italian American History and Culture* 1 (Winter 2007): 16–19. Permission was granted to the author by the *Harvard College Journal of Italian American History and Culture* to publish the full version of this paper here.

and collaborators are instrumental in advancing meaningful education in the public sphere, outside the realm of scholarly journals and the traditional classroom. Questions were established to guide the study:

1. How would you define the mission of the center/institute?
2. Who is the intended learner?
3. What are the expected outcomes of your programming?
4. What can you share about your successes and failures?
5. What is your vision for the Institute for the next three to five years?
6. How do you envision future collaboration with similar institutes in New York, New Jersey, and Pennsylvania?
7. How do you take teaching out of the classroom through the institute's programming?
8. What is your pedagogical vision for teaching Italian American literature at the center?
9. What are your personal goals for the institute?
10. Might you refer to specific experiences or events that successfully bridged academia and the public?
11. How do you go about teaching Italian and Italian American studies in a public space?
12. What strategies do you use to secure an audience?
13. What criteria do you employ to select your guest speakers?
14. How do you merge the traditional classroom and infrastructure of the university with the public forum at the institute?

Additional data was obtained through research on individual institutes and centers, as well as through observations and pre- and post-assessment surveys.

The Institute for Collaborative Research and Public Humanities at The Ohio State University seeks "to promote the engagement of the humanities with the public culture beyond the university, . . . to foster experimental interdisciplinary education, [and to be a] forum for interchange among people from on and off campus and a place where the University thinks about what it does" (http://icrph.osu.edu). Its associate director, Dr. Ron Livingston, considers the function of public-minded humanistic institutes in his article "The Humanities for Cocktail Parties and Beyond" in the *Chronicle of Higher Education*:

> Luckily, my position as associate director of a humanities institute on my campus has allowed me to experiment with alternative ways of engaging students in humanistic inquiry. One of the institute's missions is to bring students and faculty members together outside traditional classroom settings, as an antidote to the sometimes intimidating experience of attending one of the country's largest universities. Over the years we've learned that it is in such informal settings that students often begin to tie together

the different subjects they've been studying. Connecting the dots allows them to get a larger picture of the education they've been receiving. (B5)

I would like to suggest that many Italian American institutes adopt a similar methodology, seeking daily to educate students and the general public in a nonthreatening environment, using methodologies often quite different from those employed in the college classroom.

When first I conceived the title of my paper, "Modern Agoras," I meant to evoke the original meaning of the word, "a gathering space or place of congregation." The term later came to signify a marketplace and public square, the backdrop for commercial, civic, social, and religious activities. In much the same way, Italian American institutes historically have suffered from a reputation as centers of pop culture, rarely receiving credit for teaching Italian American studies in any real or rigorous way. The four centers considered in this paper, all based on university campuses, negotiate the fine line between "public gathering space" for diversion and cultural affairs and centers of intellectual discourse and inquiry. I use the term "agora" then in much the same way that Fred Gardaphè speaks of a "virtual piazza" or Anthony Tamburri a *"punto di ritrovo"* for scholars and the public alike, for though the agora was the center of public activity, Socrates himself haunted the space, lecturing to anyone willing to listen.

As the founding director of the Coccia Institute, I had the good fortune of conferring with the university and institute board of directors, comprised of faculty and external members of the local business community, on the development of the institute's mission. As stated in its guiding principles, the Coccia Institute "actively advances the growing interest in Italian and Italian American fields of study, both among scholars and the public at large. The mission of the Institute includes both academic components and public outreach, with a special focus on the historical and contemporary interplay of Italian culture and society with American culture and society." We envisioned an institute that would be recognized as the "premiere entity supporting the growth of 'emerging adults' as they learn to appreciate and contribute to Italian American culture." To achieve this mission, the institute focuses on four strategic areas: education, research, outreach, and cultural programming. With the exception of research, an area specifically designed to support scholars who are adding to the body of knowledge about Italian Americans, the activities of the institute address groups ranging from school-age children to the general public and scholarly audiences.

In much the same way, the Center for Italian Studies at Stony Brook University, led by director Dr. Mario Mignone, has three specific purposes:

. . . first, to stimulate interdisciplinary research on the part of the local academic community on issues that bring about a better understanding

of Italy and Italian Americans; second, to become a national and international focus for Italian and Italian American affairs; third, to promote
a better understanding of Italy and of Italian Americans by bringing to
the general public the latest scholarly findings on Italy and Italian Americans and by organizing cultural activities of general interest. (http://
www.italianstudies.org/center)

Its charter requires the center to organize and sponsor conferences and
lectures intended to disseminate to the public scholarly findings and to
exchange ideas. Activities include annual conferences on "Italy Today"
and Italian Americans in a multicultural society, and one-week seminars
and workshops focused on recent problems on the Italian and European
political scene and the Italian American experience.

As noted before, Dr. Anthony Tamburri, dean of The John D. Calandra
Italian American Institute at Queens College, regards the institute as a
"kind of 'punto di ritrovo,' a meeting place for our CUNY paesani: Italians,
Italian Americans, and all others interested in things 'Italian'!" (http://
qcpages.qc.cuny.edu/calandra). The institute serves to the community
a wide array of programs, from the "Philip V. Cannistraro Seminar Series
in Italian American Studies" to the film series "Documented Italians: Recent Documentary Films and Videos about Italian Americans," and the
"Writers Read" series.

The Hofstra Italian American Experience Lecture Series, under the
aegis of the Hofstra Cultural Center, carries a twofold mission, devised
by their principal funder, The Order of the Sons of Italy: to confront negative stereotypes of Italian Americans and to bring the latest scholarship
on Italy and Italian America to the public. Its director, Dr. Stanislao
Pugliese, anticipates the opportunity to increase the visibility of Italian
American studies on and off campus through expanded library holdings
and programming that unite the general public with the Hofstra student
body. Currently, Dr. Pugliese organizes one major event per semester
that engages as wide an audience as possible. Past programs and conferences include "The Most Ancient of Minorities: History and Culture of
the Jews of Italy" (1999); "Representing Sacco and Vanzetti in Art, Literature, and Film" (2002); and "If This Is a Man: The Life and Legacy of
Primo Levi" (2002).

The four centers, which speak to an absolute need to bridge the
scholarly and public worlds, attract a diverse audience of graduate and
undergraduate students, university professors, educated adults, and
many senior citizens who take advantage of public academic programming. Blended into that core audience, according to Dr. Joseph Sciorra,
assistant director of Academic and Cultural Programming at the Calandra
Institute, are "those who identify with an Italian ethnic background and
want to see their culture reflected upon, commented on, and intellectu-
alized by scholars and writers." Most institute directors and scholars be-

lieve passionately in freeing literature from the confines of the academy and making it accessible to a larger community who might benefit most from its lessons.

All four Italian American institutes employ an interdisciplinary approach to teaching Italian and Italian American studies. Because the intended learners are, generally speaking, comprised primarily of the public, the focus tends to shift from rigorous literary analysis to a consideration of literature's role in disseminating Italian and Italian American culture. Institutes provide a forum for the lively exchange of ideas about works of nonfiction or literature discussed within an historical or cultural context. Within the domain of the virtual piazza/forum/agora, literature acts as a portal through which those outside of the ivory tower can understand and contextualize their own histories. Academic jargon, according to the institute directors, alienates the public, who often attend symposia and lectures as a means of identifying with the words of Italian American authors in a very personal way. Dr. Sciorra remarks that scholars who are able to convey complex theoretical ideas in an engaging, conversational tone receive praise from the informed Calandra Institute audience whose members expect a certain academic rigor from guest speakers.

Like the directors of the other three institutes, Dr. Pugliese organizes at Hofstra "academic events for a nonscholarly audience," a task replete with logistical challenges. "Our conferences," he states, "are schizophrenic in character," due to the theoretical nature of certain panels and the mixed audience of scholars and the public. Dr. Fred Gardaphè, former director of Stony Brook University's Italian American studies program, adds that "a literate public often will not accept an experimental writer or artist," and that we academics must devise selection criteria that result in topics that matter to the public. Moreover, it is incumbent upon scholars to lead such events in order to present and explain cutting-edge art and literature to the nonacademic audience. "We are responsible," he comments, "for expanding the notion of Italian Americanness and for attracting new generations to our literature." Dr. Joseph Sciorra, a folklorist and ethnographer, concurs: "We can perform public service while theorizing about what we are doing, thereby engendering additional scholarship on topics of Italian American studies."

The Chronicle of Higher Education regularly publishes articles with titles that reflect the need for public scholarship. In "Taking Public Scholarship Seriously," Nancy Cantor and Steven D. Lavine describe the ways in which scholars and artists increasingly engage in public scholarship by:

> . . . leaving their campuses to collaborate with their communities, [exploring] such multidisciplinary issues as citizenship and patriotism, ethnicity and language, space and place, and the cultural dimensions of health and religion. They are creating innovative methods and vocabu-

laries for scholarship using cutting-edge technology, pursuing novel kinds of creative work, and integrating research with adventurous new teaching strategies. (B20)

In his article "Humanities Scholars Debate Whether Anyone is Listening to Them," Richard Bryne shares findings from a panel on "The Humanities and Its Publics" at the American Council of Learned Societies annual meeting in 2005. The debate about the "dire state of academic publishing . . . and an even more basic reexamination of the mission of the disciplines themselves" engaged representatives of organizations that, much like the institutes mentioned here, "straddle academe and the public sphere" (Byrne A15). Panelist David Marshall, a professor of English and dean of the Humanities and Fine Arts at the University of California at Santa Barbara, argued the existence of a "misalignment" between the humanities and the public, noting that increased public fascination with educational cable programming on the History Channel and the Discovery Channel "signaled an 'appetite' for humanistic discourse that remained generally unsatisfied by academics," while Jean Bethke Elshtain, professor of Social and Political Ethics in the Divinity School at the University of Chicago, blamed the academy for the "perceived public deficit in the humanities" (Bryne A15). Elshtain offered a model of scholarly public engagement as practiced by Jane Addams, a nineteenth-century social activist who provided to working-class Chicago residents a library, evening classes, and an art gallery through her central project, Hull House (Bryne A15). "If we speak clearly and honestly," said Dr. Elshtain of the public, "they will listen. They are out there" (Bryne A15). Robert Weisbuch, former president of the Woodrow Wilson National Fellowship Foundation and current president of Drew University, argued that the United States was laboring under a simultaneous "cultural boom and academic bust," and that "it is not the world that has refused the humanities; it is the humanities that have refused the world" (Bryne A15). "Reconsidering that choice," he insisted, "should be the chief duty of a new generation of scholars" (Bryne A15).

Though Italian American institutes based on university campuses have only scratched the surface of what needs to be done to address the larger question of public education, they follow Jane Addams in their collective mission to provide literary programming to the community at large. Dr. Mary Jo Bona, professor of Italian American Studies and English at Stony Brook, refuses to "talk around literature" at events sponsored by the university's Center for Italian Studies. Bona still gives intellectual, readerly presentations, but she makes the literature accessible to her audience by ending in the oral tradition. "We might read and discuss a poem by Maria Mazziotti Gillan," Bona explains, "for the future of Italian American Studies lies in literature, not in pop culture." Bona firmly believes that we must continue at all costs to "get people together to read.

This must be a part of what we do," she urges. "We must constantly remember why we went into the field: for our love of language and literature." Stressing the critical importance of a constantly exercised "reading habit," Bona references the burgeoning program for readers in America, the book club. Sparked by Oprah's Book Club in 1996, the trend has grown significantly over the past decade. Bona proposes that scholars must emphasize the difference between popular literature and literary texts, while giving the American public permission to take part in a book club. In January 2006, the Coccia Institute at Montclair State University launched its Italian American Book Club for the community at large. The club meets at the Coffee Club in Montclair, New Jersey for "coffee, biscotti, and a good read." Selected by the group leader and writer Luisa Matarazzo, with input from members of the club, featured authors include Paolo Paolicelli, Adriana Trigiani, Marianna De Marco Torgovnick, Matthew Pearl, Edvige Giunta, Louise DeSalvo, Rita Ciresi, Kym Ragusa, Helen Barolini, and Robert Viscusi, among others.

The small sample of institutes considered for this article makes evident the valuable work accomplished daily at academic Italian American institutes and centers in and around New York City. The next stage of my research will bring me to the doorstep of the highly successful Casa Italiana Zerilli-Marimò at New York University, an institute established with a generous endowment from the Baroness Zerilli-Marimò and directed by Dr. Stefano Albertini. In addition, I have initiated a conversation with the Center for Italian Studies at the University of Pennsylvania, an academic center of excellence guided by a board of university scholars who represent a multitude of disciplines. Though both institutes concentrate primarily on Italian studies, the growing field of Italian American studies is reflected in their recent programming.

As the audience at Italian American institutes grows, the academic work and theory of scholars will naturally receive more exposure. In this way, if in no other, public work enhances our scholarship. We must all work creatively and engage in the balancing act of serving two equally important crowds: the academy and the public. "Be more generous as scholars," Dr. Sciorra exhorts. "Once upon a time," he remembers, "we would hold onto our information as a source of power. That time is gone. Now we need to share."

Works Cited

Bona, Mary Jo. Telephone Interview with Gina Miele. 18 Dec. 2006.

Bryne, Richard. "Humanities Scholars Debate Whether Anyone Is Listening to Them." *The Chronicle of Higher Education: Research & Publishing* 20 May 2005 (LI, 37): A15.

Cantor, Nancy, and Steven Lavine. "Taking Public Scholarship Seriously." *The Chronicle of Higher Education Review* 9 June 2006 (LII, 40): B20.

Center for Italian Studies, Stony Brook University. http://www.italianstudies.org/center.

Gardaphè, Fred. Telephone Interview with Gina Miele. 7 Dec. 2006.

Institute for Collaborative Research and Public Humanities, Ohio State University. http://www.icrph.osu.edu.

Italian American Experience Lecture Series, Hofstra University. http://www.hofstra.edu/Community/culctr/culctr_events_italianamerican.html.

John D. Calandra Italian American Institute. http://qcpages.qc.cuny.edu/calandra/.

Joseph and Elda Coccia Institute for the Italian Experience in America, Montclair State University. http://chss.montclair.edu/cocciainstitute/.

Livingston, Ron. "The Humanities for Cocktail Parties and Beyond." *The Chronicle of Higher Education Review* 7 Jan. 2005 (LI, 18): B5.

Pugliese, Stanislao. Telephone Interview with Gina Miele. 11 Dec. 2006.

Sciorra, Joseph. Telephone Interview with Gina Miele. 4 Dec. 2006.

JOSEPH CONTE

A MAN CALLED CODY
Race and the "Passing" of a Sicilan in New Orleans

Iron Eyes Cody. His face is familiar to many as the dignified American Indian who, in a public service announcement for Keep America Beautiful first aired on Earth Day 1971, sheds a single tear for a North American environment ravaged by industrial pollutants and carelessly disposed-of litter. So memorable was this one-minute spot that "the image of the Native American, as portrayed by the actor Iron Eyes Cody," was posthumously recycled by Keep America Beautiful as "the official logo for the Great American Cleanup™ 2001" [See Figure 1]. Cody was said to have initially refused to appear in the spot because, he remarked, "[real] Indians don't cry." No less than Lady Bird Johnson apparently persuaded him to do the commercial. Indeed, he was a dedicated naturalist and a skillful archer and hunter who maintained his Moosehead Museum in the basement of his home in Los Angeles, guiding youth groups on tours of his extensive collection of Native American artifacts. An author, he published *Indian Talk: Hand Signals of the American Indians (1970); Indian Rituals*; and an autobiography, *Iron Eyes Cody: My Life as a Hollywood Indian* (1982). At his death at age 94 on January 4, 1999, he was eulogized as a distinguished actor who appeared in virtually every important Hollywood western—more than 100 films. While still a teenager, he purportedly appeared as an extra in the first truly epic western, *The Covered Wagon* (1923); then in John Ford's masterpiece *The Iron Horse* (1924); and in *The Vanishing American* (1925), a film that portrayed the near extinction of the American Indian race in Darwinian "survival of the fittest" terms. Among the tribe of actors wearing burnt sienna makeup, Cody stood out for what *The Independent on Sunday* describes as "a fine, noble face that was not 'white'" (Thomson 4). He had more substantial roles in Cecil B. DeMille's *The Plainsman* (1936) and *Unconquered* (1947). He costarred as Crazy Horse in *Sitting Bull* (1954), and

23

had prominent roles in *Kit Carson* (1940); *The Great Sioux Massacre* (1965); and *A Man Called Horse* (1970). He was usually the only "genuine American Indian" in the cast of these Hollywood epics and, as such, came to epitomize the "Red Indian" for American filmgoers. But just as the tear in the public service announcement is a glycerine fake, so also Iron Eyes Cody's racial identity has been falsified.

According to an investigative report by film scholar Angela Aleiss in the *New Orleans Times-Picayune* (26 May 1996), "Native Son," Cody was born Oscar DeCorti on April 3, 1904, in the small town of Kaplan, Louisiana. Baptismal records at Holy Rosary Catholic Church in Louisiana's Vermilion parish show that his sponsors christened him "Espera," hope (*speranza*). His first transformation of identity, then, was the anglicization of his given name from "Espera" to Oscar. He was the second of four children of Antonio DeCorti, an Italian immigrant, and Francesca Salpietra, a short woman with long black hair and dark skin who grew up in Sicily among a family of winegrowers. Her traditional parents had arranged her marriage to DeCorti and sent her off to America. New Orleans passenger lists indicate that Salpietra arrived in 1902 to meet her waiting fiancé. Cody had long claimed in his autobiography and in other publicity statements that he had been born in the Oklahoma Territory to a father, Thomas Long Plume, who was a Cherokee Indian, and a mother, Frances Salpet, who was Cree. His father, he said, had performed in Wild West shows and circuses, and after taking the family to Hollywood, served as a technical adviser on early westerns. The mask of his racial identity was lifted by Cody's half sister, May Abshire, when she was interviewed by Aleiss, who wanted to document the career of the famous Native American actor. Abshire surprisingly revealed that Cody's parents were not Cherokee or Cree, but that he was a full-blooded Italian.

What were the motivations for DeCorti-Cody's transformation of his racial identity, and why would he fix on a cultural exchange from Sicilian to Cherokee? Abshire recalls that as a boy, Oscar "always said he wanted to be an Indian. If he could find something that looked Indian, he'd put it on" (Aleiss, "Native Son"). Most of us harbor youthful fantasies of becoming something that we are not, especially something more romantic and illustrious than what we suspect we have already become. For most, these fantasies pass with maturity, but it must be a powerful compulsion that would sustain such private and public deception for nearly eighty years. A prominent factor in DeCorti's self-fashioned transformation may be found in the harsh climate of deprivation and outright hostility that greeted Italian immigrants to New Orleans at the turn of the last century. DeCorti's parents arrived in New Orleans only a decade after the notorious lynching of eleven Italian immigrants in 1891. According to James Elbert Cutler, in *Lynch-Law: An Investigation into the History of Lynching in the United States* (1905):

On March 14, 1891, the eleven Italians who were accused of complicity in the murder of the chief of police of New Orleans were summarily put to death by a mob . . . . Italy demanded from the United States an indemnity for the lynching of the Italians at New Orleans. Foreign newspapers and periodicals united in heaping abusive censure upon the United States. (228–29)

It's now virtually forgotten that the mass lynching of the Italians nearly triggered a war between the United States and Italy. There were several other incidents of racial violence toward Italian immigrants in the deep South, both before and after 1900. The NAACP, in its report *Thirty Years of Lynching in the United States, 1889–1918* (1919), records the New Orleans riot as well as the August 9, 1896 lynching of three Italians in Halumlee, Louisiana for murder. In his stunning pictorial history, *Without Sanctuary: Lynching Photography in America* (2000), James Allen includes two photographs of the lynching of Castenego Ficcarotta and Angelo Albano, September 20, 1910, in Tampa, Florida. Ficcarotta and Albano were cigar factory workers accused of shooting J. F. Esterling, a bookkeeper, during a labor strike. Ficcarotta is mockingly posed with a pipe clenched in his teeth, perhaps as a sign of his trade, or more likely in derision of his Italian heritage.

Oscar DeCorti's parents encountered the racial prejudice of the New Orleans white population for its "nonwhite" residents. May Abshire recalls her mother telling the children, "We were known as 'Dagoes' (knives) when we got there" (Aleiss, "Native Son"). Ida B. Wells, in her pamphlet *Mob Rule in New Orleans* (1900), provides an account of a New Orleans race riot in 1900 in which two black men were murdered by the New Orleans police, calling the incident "the bloodiest week which New Orleans has known since the massacre of the Italians" (5). Abshire recounts that Francesca and Antonio DeCorti soon left New Orleans to work in Louisiana's sugar cane fields, where Sicilian immigrants commonly replaced black slave labor. As freed slaves and their descendents left the cane plantations for more promising work in cities such as St. Louis or Chicago in the late nineteenth century, the exhausting manual labor of cutting cane fell to the newest arrivals from southern Europe. Sicilians were not only replacement labor for the departing Negroes, they were treated to the same brand of justice as the freed slaves. In Louisiana in 1905, the "color line" grouped Italian immigrants with other nonwhite peoples.

In *Lynch Law,* Cutler provides a "Chart of the Number of Whites, Negroes and Others Lynched According to Years 1882–1903." He reports that the "total number of Negroes lynched during the twenty-two years is 2,060," and the "total number of whites lynched during the twenty-two years is 1,169." On an annual basis, one observes the number of whites lynched—many of whom were the victims of crude frontier justice for the crimes of murder and livestock theft in western states—declining steadily from 1884 to 1903. There is an equally observable increase in the number of blacks lynched during the same period in racially moti- vated violence. Cutler concludes, "the waves for the whites and the Ne- groes do not correspond at all from year to year, but this perhaps can be explained by the fact that the lynching of Negroes is characteristic of the Southern States while the lynching of whites is characteristic of the Western States" (171). Of interest to the DeCorti family of New Orleans:

> [the chart] also shows, under the title of Others, the comparatively small number (108) of Indians, Mexicans and foreigners that have been lynched during the twenty-two years. In the years when the larger num- bers were lynched they were distributed as follows: in 1883, seven Mex- icans, four Indians, and one Chinaman; in 1884, six Mexicans, one Indian, one Japanese, and one Swiss; in 1885, six Chinese and two In- dians; in 1891, eleven Italians (at New Orleans), two Indians, and two Chinese; in 1893, five Italians, two Indians, two Mexicans, and one Bo- hemian; in 1895, five Italians (at Walsenburg, Colorado), two Indians, and two Mexicans. In all, forty-five Indians, twenty-eight Italians, twenty Mexicans, twelve Chinese, one Japanese, one Swiss, and one Bohemian were lynched during the period 1882–1903. (171–72)

Writing in 1905, and with obvious revulsion toward the practice of lynching, Cutler sees no contradiction in grouping Italians with the "Oth- ers" in his chart, among peoples who are neither whites nor blacks. Al- though I am not quite sure what to make of the motivation for the lynching of the lone Bohemian, it's clear that the Italians were victims of racially motivated violence. Cutler points out, in pursuit of his regional hypothesis for *Lynch Law,* that "in the Southern Group of States more than three times as many Negroes as whites have been lynched. In Texas the 'Others' were Mexicans, with the exception of one Indian; in Louisiana the 'Others' were all Italians" (181).

It is true that the number of lynchings of American Indians in the United States at the turn of the century somewhat exceeds that of Ital- ians. And yet, for an Italian immigrant in Louisiana, the possibility of meeting with racially motivated violence either in New Orleans or on the plantations was not remote. The dark-skinned Sicilians had assumed many of the occupations recently vacated by blacks. They worked as col- oreds, and were treated as colored. How is it, then, that the raven- haired, dark-eyed DeCorti, who would not have been able to "pass" as "white" in the New Orleans of his birth, was able to "pass" as an Amer- ican Indian, apparently without question, for years? It would be ridicu- lous not to suggest that he looked the part. With the long black hair and dark complexion inherited from his mother, an aquiline nose, and rugged jaw, Oscar DeCorti costumed as an Indian Chieftain meets every stereo-typical image of the Noble Savage. DeCorti's transformation into a Plains Indian may have been an act of escapism, exchanging a maligned iden-tity as a "dago" for the romantic vision of an Indian "brave" in the Amer-ican west. As the actual threat from Indian uprisings in the territories was eliminated and Native Americans were entirely confined to reserva-tions, the process of fictionalizing the settling of the West—dignifying the white settlers in their conflicts with a resolute if murderous indigenous population—took over. According to Thomson and the *Los Angeles Times* obituary, Cody is either said to have made his film debut as a child in D. W. Griffith's *The Massacre* (1913) or as an Indian dancer when a Para-mount Pictures crew used his family's farm for location shooting in 1919.[1] DeCorti escaped a dismal and penurious future of withering agricultural labor. His self-fashioning of a Plains Indian identity would coincide with America's need to depict in self-flattering terms the inexorable conquest of the west in the Hollywood western.

After the early death of his debt-ridden father, Oscar DeCorti left Louisiana with his two brothers, Joseph and Frank, in search of better prospects. All three brothers changed their name from Corti to Cody when they arrived among the citrus groves of southern California. It was then that Iron Eyes "turned 100 percent Indian," as his half sister puts it. "He had his mind all the time on movies" (Aleiss, "Native Son"). With his fea-tures it was unlikely that Cody would play any leading man roles in the Hollywood film industry. Options for Italian ethnic parts were rather limited for Cody/DeCorti to supporting roles in gangster films; in effect, he would have had to play the very knife-wielding dago whose stereotype he had left Louisiana to avoid. America had cast the Italian as a murderous crim-inal, but Cody/DeCorti refused to play that part. As Iron Eyes Cody, he made a living by performing in the only role permitted to a dark-complex-ioned male in the Hollywood film industry in the 1930s and 1940s. As an Indian dancer in Zane Grey's *The Golden West* (1932); as the Shoshone Chief in *Kit Carson* (1940); and as Crazy Horse in *Sitting Bull* (1954), Cody had at least the possibility of a dramatic role with some dignity.

Oscar DeCorti's "passing" as a Native American raises the question of the relation between race and ethnicity in a culture that prefers not to distinguish too finely between Sicilian immigrants and the descendents of freed slaves. It's much easier for a person of color to be mistaken for a person of nearly any other color than it is for that person of color to pass as "white." Espera DeCorti transformed himself into Oscar Corti and then into Iron Eyes Cody, and no one questioned his race or ethnicity for decades; but neither did anyone confuse him with Clark Gable in *Gone*

---

[1] As with the varying dates of birth for Cody, these claims for his film debut (the former at the age of five) are based on Cody/DeCorti's own statements. Aleiss argues that "Cody didn't appear in movies until the late 1920s" ("Wannabe Indian" 31).

With the Wind (1939). Similarly, Anthony Quinn (born Antonio Rudolfo Oaxaca Quinn, in Chihuahua, Mexico of an Irish father and Mexican mother) variously played Greeks (*The Guns of Navarone,* 1961; *Zorba the Greek,* 1964), Arabs (*Sinbad the Sailor,* 1947), Italians (in Federico Fellini's *La Strada,* 1954), Asians (as Kublai Khan in *Marco the Magnificent,* 1965), Indians (*Buffalo Bill,* 1944), and even Mexicans (*Viva Zapata!,* 1952). One might ask why Iron Eyes Cody, when confronted with his half sister's revelations, denied his "white" "European" heritage, stating, "You can't prove it. . . . All I know is that I'm just another Indian." But what other part could Oscar DeCorti play in the saga of American ethnicity?

Figure 1: Iron Eyes Cody in *Keep America Beautiful PSA*

Works Cited

Aleiss, Angela. "Native Son." *New Orleans Times-Picayune* 26 May 1996: D1.

___. "Iron Eyes Cody: Wannabe Indian." *Cineaste* 25 (Dec. 1999): 30–31.

Allen, James, et al. *Without Sanctuary: Lynching Photography in America.* Santa Fe, NM: Twin Palms, 2000.

Anonymous obituary. "Iron Eyes Cody, Memorable Indian Actor, Dies at 94." *Los Angeles Times* 5 Jan. 1999: B1.

Cutler, James Elbert. *Lynch-Law: An Investigation into the History of Lynching in the United States.* 1905. Montclair, NJ: Patterson Smith, 1969.

The NAACP. *Thirty Years of Lynching in the United States, 1889–1918.* 1919. New York: Negro Universities P, 1969.

Thomson, David. "Real Indians Don't Cry. So Why Did Iron Eyes Cody?" *The Independent on Sunday* (London, England) 10 Jan. 1999: 4.

Wells-Barnett, Ida B. *On Lynchings: Southern Horrors, A Red Record, and Mob Rule in New Orleans.* New York: Arno Press and the *New York Times,* 1969.

ROSEANNE GIANNINI QUINN

LANGUAGE, REVOLUTION, AND ITALIAN AMERICAN IDENTITY IN THE CROSS-GENRE WRITING OF CAROLE MASO

The book opens on August 15; the story takes place in one day. Its characters are Italian American. The narrative moves back and forth in time. Sometimes it is difficult to know who is talking, because maybe no one is, because the words may just represent thoughts or memories of a particular character or are simply examples of artistic fortitude. The concluding section of this book, entitled "The Present Moment," is deliberately obscure. Throughout the text, there are meditations on the illusiveness of literary representation. Consider this passage:

> You want a why. But there is no why. . . . These are the faces of the friends I knew there, but no such depiction is forthcoming, too bad, no artifacts by which in later years to verify that I was there and my recollections are credible, no way to disprove your suspicion that I simply was, then was not, and now am again since I departed the train onto the platform. I want to be that line that extends and ravels and at length intersects itself again, a path that can be retraced stepwise, but I am not, I am discontinuous. (Scibona 198)

This book is not *AVA,* not *The American Woman in the Chinese Hat,* not *The Art Lover,* not even *Ghost Dance.* Rather, it is the *The End,* by Salvatore Scibona, a finalist for the 2008 National Book Award. Repeatedly in reviews, this writer is compared to Virginia Woolf, James Joyce, William Faulkner, and Saul Bellow. He is never once compared to Carole Maso to whom he seems such an obvious contemporary literary descendant. That has much more to do, of course, with the legacy of mainstream criticism ignoring Maso than it has to do with anything else.

Carole Maso, author of six novels including *Ghost Dance* (1986), *The Art Lover* (1990), *AVA* (1993), *The American Woman in the Chinese Hat* (1994), *Defiance* (1999), and *Aureole* (2003), has in recent years turned her considerable writing talents explicitly toward exploring the memoir form with her series of three books: *The Room Lit by Roses: A Journal of Pregnancy and Birth* (2000); *Break Every Rule: Essays on Language, Longing, & Moments of Desire* (2000); and *Beauty is Convulsive: The Passion of Frida Kahlo* (2002). Each of these books incorporates biographical aspects of Maso's life: daughter of an Italian American father, partner to her beloved Helen, and mother to her daughter Rose, but also each memoir opens a window onto her fiction writing that has variously been described as experimental, ecstatic, postmodern, and avant-garde. In this essay, I wish to examine Maso's particular importance as a literary innovator, blurring formal boundaries of memoir, fiction, and literary criticism, from the theoretical perspective of her as a distinctly Italian American feminist writer.

When examining a range of her books, read across blurred genres, Maso both complicates the memoir form and demystifies her fiction, not so much to expose artifice but to reveal process. In one of Maso's essays from *Break Every Rule,* entitled "Notes of a Lyric Artist Working in Prose: A Lifelong Conversation with Myself Entered Midway," she layers the representation of (overheard) cultural memory and creative (non)intentionality:

> . . . Helen reading my father the recipe for ravioli dough. He remembers his family drying pasta on the beds in the Brooklyn house of his childhood. "Dig a well. Then put in eggs." And I type it directly into the text of *AVA,* which I am working on in the next room. A place for the random, the accidental, the overheard, the incidental. *Precious, disappearing things. (Break* 29)

Of course, this passage is a commentary on the disappearing rituals of Italian American culture and how often the third generation must construct family narrative and tradition in haphazard ways. But it also calls to mind that such Italian American cultural "disappearances" are rendered by Maso over and over again in her work, in a nostalgic postmodern pastiche, if you will, precisely in order to enact an Italian American cultural aesthetic.

When opening the pages of *The Room Lit By Roses,* at first, it looks like a typical diary-driven account of a woman's pregnancy. There are long, connected paragraphs, divided into sections by date. But then the passages begin to fragment; paragraphs are disrupted, and discordant lines appear. Some of those lines are directly from her novels; sometimes Maso will tell you where the lines come from; other times, the reader might actually know without being told. The intertextuality can function almost like a woman's classic *secret* diary. For example, when she suddenly asks a seemingly nonsensical question, "How are you feeling, Ava Klein?" an experienced Maso reader will know all about the answer to that question, which is "Not very well and about to die," from reading the novel *AVA.* This type of literal code-cracking parallels the rule-breaking content in *The Room Lit by Roses.*

Maso's is one of the few literary memoirs that describes the experiences of a lesbian giving birth (another notable account is Cherrié Moraga's *Waiting in the Wings: Portrait of a Queer Motherhood*). The kinds of hetero-normative pressures that are directed at Maso extend from her relationship with Helen, to childbearing, to the act of writing itself. As such, and by necessity, she explains, "This child was created outside the usual constraints and enclosures, without the usual prescriptions, hierarchies, sentences leveled at her head" (*Room* 30). Still, despite her lesbian identification, the fact that she is a pregnant woman gives her status as she moves through the world. Not quite jokingly, Maso writes of the approval she receives from the staff women at her university. When they discover that she is pregnant, Maso realizes, "I don't seem like such a complete oddball to the secretaries at Brown anymore" (*Room* 96). Throughout her memoir, she does not just comment on the mainstream views held about her life; she also repeatedly refers to the ways in which her analogous "oddball" writing style has been received by the New York literary establishment.

In this regard, the implications of Maso's transgressions are more fully examined by her in *Break Every Rule.* What happens to a woman writer who lives outside convention and writes in a way that goes unsanctioned and is, quite frankly, often not well understood? In the mainstream publishing world, she tells us, her manuscripts still lie actually and metaphorically dormant, "in your disdainful box labeled 'experimental.' Labeled 'do not open.' Labeled 'do not review'" (*Break* 165). In this way, Maso's work, I think, can be read as a differing counter-narrative. In her important essay entitled "The New World of Italian American Studies," Josephine Gattuso Hendin has a section on the now well-known impact of biased anti-immigration and intermarriage laws directed at Italian Americans in the early part of the twentieth century. She speaks of that period of time in literary terms, stating that, for Italian Americans, ". . . even laws served as narratives of rejection" (155).

In this sense, Maso does not mask her project; after all, she calls her book *Break Every Rule* in the first place, and it clearly reads from the starting point of outsiderness. Maso has also been sorely underestimated for the way in which her destabilizing of narrative in her memoirs is also meant to call for social revolutionary change. She asks:

> Would disrupting or upsetting the lexical surfaces, the deeper structures
> disrupt other contracts (social, political) we have entered with those who

have continually tried to dismiss us? . . .

Might the old novel, one day, like the old ways of thinking about gender and race and sexuality, simply appear silly, outdated, quaint? (*Break* 159–60)

As Maso has literally experienced rejection as a lesbian, a lesbian mother, and a genre-blurring storyteller, there is no avenue that exists besides resistive lawbreaking.

In general, Maso herself is not talked about as an Italian American subject. Within the limited attention that has been paid to her by mainstream literary critics, none of them write about her ethnic lyrical sensibilities except for critics who are themselves Italian American. From her first novel, *Ghost Dance,* Maso's work has been studied and embraced by Italian American scholars in two significant ways: (1) for her literary contributions to innovative narrative; (2) for her complex articulations of cultural hybridity and the varied dilemmas of representing ethnic identity that is so often found in texts by third-generation non-Anglo ethnic writers and by writers of color in the United States. Fred Gardaphè, in his now classic study *Italian Signs, American Streets,* for example, explains:

> Maso presents the experience of the third-generation ethnic who, unlike earlier generations, has the option of picking and choosing from the many traditions that make up American culture. In *Ghost Dance,* Carole Maso depicts the results of stitching a self together out of disparate parts. (149)

Gardaphè's analysis of *Ghost Dance* works equally as well when applied to the book *AVA.* Maso's picking and choosing of seemingly disparate fragmentary details of the last day and memories of her character's life, which also occur on August 15, the Catholic feast day of the assumption of Mary, interspersed with historical accounts of the first Gulf War, random newspaper headlines, the AIDS epidemic, decaying Italian piazzas, and the Holocaust of World War II, combined with interstices in the text of blank spaces, simulating silences, followed by actual quotes from living and dead feminist writers and theorists create what I would call a feminist ethnic postmodernism. Maso writes of Ava:

> She sits at the edge of the bed.
> Her voice, the free world. (*AVA* 258)

Cumulatively, however, the settling along side, refusing to hierarchize, is not without its critical literary consequences. In her recent and important essay entitled "'Treblinka, a rather musical word': Carole Maso's Post-Holocaust Narrative," scholar Robin Silbergleid writes of the book: "There are, no doubt, readers who would find Maso's use of the Holocaust reprehensible" (2). In Silbergleid's analysis, as she describes it, "*AVA* is, in the most basic sense of the term, a post-Holocaust text: a novel written in the wake of the Holocaust and affected by it in both content and form" (2). One of the dilemmas she engages with is that Maso, as neither a Holocaust survivor nor a descendant of one, may have an ethical responsibility not to employ the Holocaust as a metaphor, a backdrop, an imaginative setting, a history for her character whose Aunt Sophie is murdered by the Nazis. It is a literary-experiential debate that is not unfamiliar. Can and should writers from one racial or ethnic background create characters and worlds across such boundaries beyond their own experience and/or cultural legacies? Silbergleid ultimately answers "yes" to that question, and she is the first literary critic to give such a full accounting of the book's significance in this context.

As understood in this way, then, the double ethnic consciousness of *AVA,* Italian American and Jewish American, now also seems impossible for me not to see as purposefully nostalgic. Italian American cultural clues abound in the novel, while Jewish history forms its core. Perhaps the lesson of ethnic postmodernism looks, in Maso's case, a lot like what is learned from the feminist concept of intersectionality. Holding up for view the idea that a person can embody more than one subject position at the same time allows for an appreciation of identity as multiple on the one hand—and for the expression of a multivalent storyteller, both as a recorder of truthful and imagined memory, on the other. Ava the character is in a constant state of loss and longing: her dead aunt, her dying self, the memory of her many male lovers, the missed opportunity to be in Italy in love with the women there, being written onto and, ultimately, off of the end of the page with her death from a rare blood disease. Maso, in many prose commentaries on how to read her work, maintains that it is the reader who ultimately creates the narrative (*Break* 70–71).

In the recent collection of prose and poetry edited by the late Reginald Shepard entitled *Lyric Postmodernisms,* Peter Gizzi reflects on his own avant-garde writing as creating a "condition of openness" that "is both a construction of self and an emptying of self—not autobiographical but autographical—flexible enough to accommodate figures, things, voices, documentation: to combine, build and dissolve being, boundaries—to somehow let the poem become itself" (86). It is at this flexible juncture, I think, where reader and writer connect to push against the margin and spaces of Maso's texts. It is where the experience of reading all of Maso's work, at her own urging invitation, loosens the grip of mere nostalgia, the desire for lost cultural identity, toward the freedom of reimagining the meaning of memory and thereby transforming it in infinite ways.

In turn, the recognition of ethnicity, too, in a "condition of openness" can exist, not as some tired post-referential state of mind, but as both lived and imagined experience. As we let ourselves become ourselves, whatever our embodied identification, that state of openness hopefully allows for a kind of liberation of the voices of the text(s): where that which is both present and silent more fully speak.

Throughout Maso's work, she reimagines possibilities of life, what a woman can be, and life writing, not just what a novel or a memoir can look like but what work can look like for a literary artist. Perhaps this is one of her greatest contributions: a revitalized state of lyric prose of post-nostalgia, ultimately beyond decay and toward the preservation of an Italian American literary heritage that we can call our own. In terms of the idea and praxis of innovation, though, it has been more than twenty years since Maso emerged as a distinctly new voice ringing in our consciousness; that is a long time now. Still, however, she continues to push toward future, broader incantations. In an interview in *The Barcelona Review,* Maso explains:

> I'm just not interested in writing books that resemble other books any-more. . . . I am interested in combining more completely and convinc-ingly disparate forms: essay, poetry, and the visual arts with the fiction. I am interested in dissolving character and working more in multi-voiced, polyphonic sheets of sound. . . . . All the while re-imagining for myself what narrative is, and how to keep a grounding element present in some way. I am not interested in writing inscrutable texts, but ones that will engage me and enlarge my notions of what is possible. ... I think a book is capable of almost anything. I don't think we've even scratched the surface yet. (Adams np).

For Italian Americans, long affected by modes of Anglo admonishment as well as by academic and literary marginalization, Carole Maso's innovative prose keeps a persisting presence that remains impossible to ignore. At the same time, she recodes an expansive multigenerational storytelling, where, as she explains, ". . . it is not the form but the fact that *you are the form* that is important" (*Break* 101).

About his novel *The End,* Salvatore Scibona tells us that his own mode of writing has been heavily influenced by musical lyricism. Or, as Ava tells us:

> Through the clearing in these exciting and dangerous woods,
> Where I hear you,
> Singing,
> . . .
> The irresistible music of the end.
> Libera me.
> Turn it up.
> You're exactly as I remember you.

Fly.

How is this for an ending? (AVA 174-5)

Works Cited

Adams, Jill. "Interview with Carole Maso." *The Barcelona Review* 20 (Sept.-Oct. 2000): np. www.barcelonareview.com.

Gardaphè, Fred. *Italian Signs, American Streets: The Evolution of Italian American Narrative.* Durham, NC: Duke UP, 1996.

Gizzi, Peter. "Artist's Statement." *Lyric Postmodernisms: An Anthology of Contemporary Innovative Poetries.* Ed. Reginald Shepard. Denver, CO: Counterpoint, 2008. 85–86.

Hendin, Josephine Gattuso. "The New World of Italian American Studies." *American Literary History* 13.1 (Mar. 2001): 141–57.

Maso, Carole. *The American Woman in the Chinese Hat.* Normal, IL: Dalkey Archive P, 1994.

____. *The Art Lover.* Hopewell, NJ: Ecco, 1990.

____. *AVA.* Normal, IL: Dalkey Archive P, 1993.

____. *Break Every Rule: Essays on Language, Longing, & Moments of Desire.* Washington, DC: Counterpoint, 2000.

____. *Beauty is Convulsive: The Passion of Frida Kahlo.* Washington, DC: Counterpoint, 2002.

____. *Ghost Dance.* San Francisco, CA: North Point P, 1986.

____. *The Room Lit by Roses: A Journal of Pregnancy and Birth.* Washington, DC: Counterpoint, 2000.

Moraga, Cherríe. *Waiting in the Wings: Portrait of a Queer Motherhood.* New York: Firebrand, 1997.

Scibona, Salvatore. *The End.* Saint Paul, MN: Graywolf, 2008.

Silbergleid, Robin. "'Treblinka, a rather musical word': Carole Maso's Post-Holocaust Narrative." *Modern Fiction Studies* 53.1 (Spring): 2007. 1–25.

JIM COCOLA

"UPSETTIN DA SETUPPA"
Vincent Ferrini's Vernacular Poetics

In the following pages, I turn to the underappreciated career of Vincent
Ferrini (1913–2007), an Italian American poet from Essex County, Massachusetts, who proved instrumental in cementing the immensely pro-
ductive correspondence between Robert Creeley and Charles Olson, and
whose poetics rest at the base of Olson's theories on composition by
field, open form, and projective verse. Having addressed Ferrini in his
first poem of his epic *Maximus* sequence, "I, Maximus of Gloucester, to
You," Olson subsequently cast him as a villainous careerist disconnected
from matters of local concern. Yet it was Ferrini's example that initially
prompted Olson to defend the importance of a poet's "own lang., syntax
and song both," in an early letter to Creeley.[1]

While Olson's promotion of the poet's idiolect might seem like a primarily or even purely aesthetic consideration, these aesthetics were but-
tressed and finally upheld by his fundamental interest in the cultural
inflections of dialect and vernacular prosodies. Indeed, the cultural dimensions of Olson's open form poetics can be read through various descent lines in American poetry, whether through his own Irish and
Swedish registers, or the French and Spanish registers of William Carlos
Williams, or the African register of Amiri Baraka, or, indeed, in the Italian—and more specifically, Abruzzese—register that finally came to Ferrini in late career.

Thus, if Olson's subsequent attack on Ferrini's poetic practices reflected Olson's own anxieties about authenticity, careerism, and identity,

---

[1] See Olson's "I, Maximus of Gloucester, to You," and "Letter 5," in *The Maximus Poems* 5;
20–29; Charles Olson, in a letter to Robert Creeley of April 21, 1950, from Washington DC,
rep. in *Charles Olson and Robert Creeley: The Complete Correspondence* I.19. For more on
the Ferrini-Olson relationship, see Clark 168; 179–80.

such anxieties were largely due to the fact that Olson, like Ferrini, was both a transplant to Cape Ann and the child of transplants in America.[2] There is a certain irony in the fact that Olson's gargantuan epic, *The Maximus Poems* (1983), emerged from a latecomer to Gloucester, and this irony was redoubled in Olson's enduring engagements with early American history and the founding history of the United States, coming as they did from a relative latecomer to the continent. After Olson's project was cut short and left unfinished after his untimely death in 1970, the field was opened to other poets that could be considered stakeholders within the Gloucester scene.

From this moment forward, Ferrini felt freer to commence work in the vein of the model he once referred to as his "absentee patrona," taking up a "big Gloucester poem" of his own, which ultimately ran to seven volumes and a thousand pages, collectively titled *Know Fish* (1979–91).[3] Like Olson, Ferrini was the child of working-class immigrants, and like Olson, Ferrini was "from away," coming to reside permanently in Gloucester only in later life. But whereas, for Ferrini, Olson spoke "to the intellectuals and the academic world," Ferrini himself spoke "to the non-poetry reader, the man on the street," and came "to him and her loaded."[4] As such, if the ethnic, immigrant character of Olson's *Maximus* is often difficult to discern, Ferrini's work is replete with ethnic material, and nowhere more prominently than in Book II of *Know Fish,* a 250-page sequence in Italian American vernacular titled "Da Songs" (1979).

Born to an Abruzzese father and a Basilicatan mother newly immigrated from Italy, Ferrini's education was defined by his status as a child of ethnic immigrants from very distinct regions of Italy. Straddling the disparate dialect traditions of his maternal and paternal lines, he necessarily assumed a fragmentary, hybridized, tentative approach to the early acquisition of English. "Words come hard and eely," Ferrini later recalled of his childhood experience, "a cross between Italian and English, or one time one, another time, the other." As a result, he found himself "floundering between the Italian and the English of Pa and Ma," with the resulting speech "broken and welded together" (*Hermit* 3–4; 24–25).

---

[2] Neither Ferrini nor Olson was native to Gloucester, Ferrini having been born in Saugus, and Olson in Worcester. As such, there is a very local aspect to such anxieties about authenticity, but that same anxiety can also be read in a much wider frame, as an allegory about the insecurities of the children of ethnic immigrant traditions, out of step with the old guard in New England and, by extension, the American tradition more generally. As Warren Tallman put it, with respect to Olson's displacement of these anxieties, "when he so scathingly attacks his fellow Gloucester poet, Vincent Ferrini [. . .] Olson is warning Olson" (62).

[3] *Know Fish* 198–99, hereafter as *KF,* refers only to Volume 1 of the epic, which includes Books I and II. Ferrini's evocation of *Know Fish* as a "big Gloucester poem" is quoted in *The Whole Song* xxvi, hereafter as *WS.*

[4] In an undated letter to Paul Metcalf, quoted in Metcalf's preface to *KF,* xiii–xviii. Later in *KF,* Ferrini drew a contrast between their respective readerships, counterposing "the scholars scavenging Olson's big bang" with "the provincial mute catching up on my slang" (43).

The result of this linguistic amalgam was not dual fluency, but rather a double consciousness of disfluency. Acknowledging Italian as a "language I cannot speak" (*Hermit* 100), Ferrini also confessed that he "had trouble in English" as a student.[5]

Related to—and perhaps resulting from—these linguistic deviations were Ferrini's political deviations as an avowed champion of the working classes and a deliberate flouter of social conventions. In the majestic stream-of-consciousness infancy tableau that introduces his autobiography, Ferrini gestured toward the standardizing pressure that hovered above his nonstandard attributes, deliberately interrupting his own florid prolegomenon with "a voice out of this chaos" that declares "YOU ARE GOING TO CONFORM YOU LITTLE BASTARD, OR WE ARE GOING TO MAKE YOUR LIFE MISERABLE" (*Hermit* 2). For the most part, in essentials, Ferrini's poetic corpus conformed closely to the work of his more experimental contemporaries, written in a relatively standard English, with shifts in diction and form that accord quite closely vis-à-vis conventional shifts within late modernist and early postmodernist poetics. The one exception to this general rule comes in "Da Songs," which presents an extreme instance of nonconformity, wherein all possible standards of speech are made to conform to Ferrini's nonstandard Italian American vernacular benchmark.

"Beware of a man who changes / hees identity n race" (165), Ferrini wrote in "Da Songs," pairing a standard English line with a vernacular English line, in an ambivalent exposition of his own trajectory from immigrant's son to unassimilated laborer to ethnic remainder. As a "Cativo," or villain, per the titular formation of the first poem in "Da Songs," he positioned himself as one of "da bambini ov irritashuns," a gadfly whose emplacement and temporality produced an identity that provoked discomfort in various populations. Well aware that "eets da dame ole story / dat went on before," Ferrini stood committed to a language and a politics that were bent upon "upsettin da settupa" (119).[6]

What, it might be asked, is "da settupa" that Ferrini took to "upsettin" in "Da Songs"? For one, he set to "upsettin da settupa" of English orthography, which he reformulated into a vernacular more suited to speech as spoken by those who shared in his own class, community, and ethnic affiliations. But beyond this, in crafting an extended discourse that is at once complex, critical, and reflective, composed in the terms of Italian American vernacular, it might also be said that Ferrini set to "upsettin da settupa" of Hollywood convention, working against crude, stereotyp-

---

[5] Quoted in *WS* xv. For more on the English language acquisition of Ferrini, his contemporaries, and his successors, see Biondi.

[6] See also the note in *WS* 195–96, which explains that "cativo" as used here "suggest[s] the resistance of a bad man or bottom dog." Taking the standard Italian *cattivo* and deploying orthography after his own fashion, Ferrini's cativo strikes a playfully reflexive vernacular note.

ical stock depictions of Italian Americans as old as—and indeed even older than—the film industry itself.

While such efforts may seem sui generis at first glance, there are numerous precedents for the bad English of Ferrini's "Da Songs." Poets of Scottish and Irish heritage from Robert Burns to Paul Muldoon have worked assiduously to challenge, complicate, and reimagine the orthodox conventions of English prosody. In the United States, this mantle was taken up as early as the middle nineteenth century by poets such as James Russell Lowell and James Whitcomb Riley, who focused on the singularities of regional and rural dialects as exceptions to the standardizing rule.

An equally compelling precedent for Ferrini's approach in "Da Songs" can be found in the African American literary tradition, whose leading lights began to take the parodies of white southerners like Joel Chandler Harris and Thomas Nelson Page into their own hands during the first decades of the twentieth century. The pioneer in this vein, Paul Laurence Dunbar, was somewhat derivative in this respect. Dismissing his dialect verse as second-rate, he staked his identity as a poet on his standard works in traditional forms and meters, which the critics duly ignored in favor of his ease and skill with the varieties of black vernacular. Later exemplars in this dialect tradition, such as Claude McKay and Sterling A. Brown, grew more comfortable with the fluidities of the form, and with their own expressive potential therein. As such, Dunbar, McKay, and Brown worked not only against the banalities of Harris's Uncle Remus, but also against the longstanding cultural form of blackface minstrelsy more generally.

While Ferrini may not have drawn directly upon such precedents, he worked in what has since emerged as a parallel tradition, serving as a specific progenitor of a more general phenomenon that Evelyn Nien-Ming Ch'ien describes as "weird English," composed of "barely intelligible and sometimes unrecognizable English created through the blending of one or more languages with English" (3–4). If anything, this parallel tradition has been even less literary than its Scottish, Irish, and African American analogues.

As in the more established cases of the Scottish, Irish, and African American traditions, Italian American custodianship of the Italian American vernacular was never strictly dependent on the terms of print culture. Yet, within the modern American context, as Helen Barolini has noted, while Italian American immigrant writers struggled to craft a literary tradition in an unfamiliar language, emerging from a separate cultural heritage that functioned by and large "without a written language and a literature," African American writers of the same period were working in a familiar medium, drawing upon "the centuries of their exposure to and absorption of English" (4). Traumatic as such exposure and absorption proved, these traumas also propelled African American writers toward modes of catharsis, critique, expression, and innovation in the English language that helped enfold them within a larger literary tradition.

By contrast, even with the revelatory contributions of the Harlem Renaissance in full flower, early twentieth-century Italian American performance artists, including Farfariello (Eduardo Migliaccio) and Nofrio (Giovanni De Rosalia), pursued a more thoroughly extra-literary mode of expression. Turning to dialect, pidgin, and vernacular speech in their wildly popular *macchiette,* or character sketches, they drew upon a Neapolitan form of dramatic monologue that turned to comedy and parody in order to think through questions of cultural identity.[7] In kind, and more in line with the African American tradition, early published works in the Italian American vernacular—such as Achille Almerini's *La colonia di Dante* (1912) and Pasquale Seneca's *Il Presidente Scoppetta* (1927)—worked against mimicries and mockeries of Italian American speech by the Irish American dialect poet T.A. Daly, just as surely as works by Dunbar, McKay, and Brown worked against the mimicries and mockeries of Harris and Page.

***

Before turning in earnest to "Da Songs," I want to call attention to the protracted deferral of Italian American identity as a prominent aspect of Ferrini's poetics. Because Ferrini's identity as a poet coalesced around the depiction of representative subjectivities other than his own, they effectively served as a cryptic means of self-expression. "If you ever / want to find / me," he explained in an early found poem, "enter / the caves / of other / people" (*Infinite* 16). Ferrini's debut volume, *No Smoke* (1941), followed the model established by Edgar Lee Masters in his *Spoon River Anthology* (1915), transplanting the model of community portraiture from small-town Illinois to the urban fabric of Lynn, Massachusetts, whose industrial identity as the center of shoe manufacture had begun to erode after a series of internecine disputes between labor and management during the early twentieth century.

Masters omitted any mention of Italian Americans in *Spoon River,* and though the Italian American population of Lynn was substantial, Ferrini followed Masters' lead and essentially marginalized them in *No Smoke.* While the opening movements of the sequence treat figures from Emma Adams and Richard Ashton to Lawrence Tudor and Nancy Turner, the back of the book turns quite decidedly to Italian Americans, with four of the final eight portraits concerning figures such as Giovanni Polito and Luigi Capodilupo, a talented but frustrated teacher whose "degrees are gathering dust in the bureau" because "the School Committee refuses to appoint him" (*No Smoke* 91–92).

Throughout the 1940s, Ferrini's infrequent attention to Italian American themes, rarely codified as such, nevertheless telegraphed a sense

---

[7] For a discussion of the *macchiette,* see Tedesco, esp. pp. 358–61.

of alienation, confusion, and insecurity common to various immigrant populations at mid-century.[8] Thus in one poem Ferrini portrays a wartime laborer ostracized from his colleagues because "He doesn't agree with them / Or talk their language" (*Injunction* 29–30). Elsewhere he speaks more evocatively of the "roots of a pain" that "branched unconsciously [. . .] in an unknown country" (*Blood* 5), describing the class of tenement dwellers as "countryless / inhabitants" (*Infinite* 19). The United States is not where Ferrini's speakers come from, but rather where they "go from and come" (*Blood* 33); as he later expressed it in a fragment included in his autobiography,

We are foreigners.
Though born here. And angers rankle in the bones.
Foreigner pitted against foreigner. (71)

With Italy and the United States declared enemies during the opening stages of World War II, a sense of dual allegiance was treasonous at worst, and remained problematic for many years thereafter. As a result, Ferrini learned to tell it slant, speaking, in a poem titled "Letter to My Brother," of "the umbilical cord connects us both / to Ma and America" (*Injunction* 42–43). This biological metaphor veils the question of citizenship in the fact of maternity, with "Ma" standing metonymically for Italy, in a neat encapsulation of the *jus sanguinis/jus soli* divide that styled Ferrini an Italian citizen by blood and a US citizen by birthplace. In a related move, if Ferrini's evocation of "southern lords" (*Injunction* 39) has an explicitly American resonance in the context of Dixie, it also retains a subterranean Italian resonance in the context of the Mezzogiorno.

But Ferrini was never alone in obscuring the Italian American aspects of his poetics. Indeed, the most common critical practice has been to label him as a working-class poet rather than as an Italian American poet.[9] In mid-career, during the ferment of the 1960s, he was hailed by Walter Lowenfels as "the last surviving Proletarian Poet." As Lowenfels went on to explain, "on the lower East Side Lowell has no existence, and in the Lowell-land Ferrini has none."[10] In a subconscious moment of ethnic stereotyping, Lowenfels here implicitly interpellates the Italian American

---

[8] Ferrini evokes this alienation in his autobiography, confessing that the 1940s were a period during which "the wind of alienation" ran "through my bones" (83) but later disowning "that 'alienation' I once felt" as "only a shadow" (197).
[9] As Butterick notes in the *DLB*, it was not until 1972 that Ferrini's work was anthologized, from *No Smoke*, as that of a "ghetto" writer, in Miller.
[10] Quoted on the inside jacket flap of Ferrini's *I Have the World* (London: Fortune P, 1967). This juxtaposition may not have been accidental. In the same period, after Lowell hailed John Ciardi as an outstanding Italian American poet, Ciardi bristled at the tag, insisting that he was every bit as much of an American poet as Lowell. See Cifelli 438–39.

poet as a New Yorker, denying Ferrini membership in the city on the hill that is the Commonwealth of Massachusetts, wherein Ferrini, a native-born son, was more consistently resident than Lowell himself. Such mixed praise surely prodded at old wounds for Ferrini, who was mentored as a young man by the aristocratic and eccentric Boston Brahmin poet John Brooks Wheelwright. Upon introducing Wheelwright to his family, Ferrini was met with a curt dismissal from his father, who concluded that his son had been "born in the wrong class to be a poet" (*Hermit* 19).

As a category distinction, this conclusion has some validity with regard to the gap between Ferrini and Wheelwright themselves, but it is even more telling with regard to the gap between their respective fathers. Whereas Ferrini's father was a shoemaker, and as such was treated by his son with an unsentimental eye, Wheelwright's poem "Father" paints a very different picture of the patriarch in both content and tone. It begins:

> An East Wind asperges Boston with Lynn's sulphurous brine.
> Under the bridge of turrets my father built . . . drip multitudes
> of checker-board shadows. (n.p.)

Presumably, Wheelwright's father, Ned, did not build this bridge, but rather commissioned it; the building itself was likely erected by those more intimately acquainted with the "sulphurous brine" of Lynn, described elsewhere by Ferrini as "our laboring ancestors / and we / Who built these States" (*Tidal Wave* 7). If, to Wheelwright, it was the industrial brine of Lynn that reeked, for Ferrini the stench was a byproduct of "the miasmas of the Caste" (*Hiding One* 7), emanating from Boston.

While Ferrini gestured toward an embrace of his Italian American identity in the 1950s and 1960s, a more elaborated exploration of his subject position was not easily accomplished. This difficulty became apparent in Ferrini's extended reply to Olson, *In The Arriving* (1954), which included the following clarification about his line of descent:

> is Pico
>   Marconi
>   in my family
>
> no
>   my ancestors.
>
> everybody is in me
> &
>   I am
>   Myself
>   the abruzzan. (n.p.)

Responding to a query about his relationship to a pair of famous figures from Emilia Romagna—the former a Renaissance philosopher from Mirandola, and the latter a fin de siècle inventor from Bologna—Ferrini dissociates from these ostensible paisans in favor of more immediate family ties to an indeterminate group of unnamed ancestors, thus announcing regional ties not to the northern Italy of Emilia Romagna, but rather to the southern Italy of the Abruzzi. The implication here is that if Ferrini's Italian American identity was broached at all in the wider American culture, it was broached via recourse to northern Italian achievements in the arts and sciences, rather than to southern Italian emigrant folkways.

* * *

Beyond mere affirmation, elaborated articulations of southern Italian heritage were quite slow in coming for Ferrini. As late as 1975, his *Ten Pound Light*—later republished as the opening movement to Book III of *Know Fish*—employed orthographic formulations such as "thee & thine," and "Gloucester," and "cod" (n.p.); it was only in "Da Songs" that "thee & thine" became "ya," "Gloucester" became "Glotza," and "cod" became "bacala" (164; 171). This belated though radical turn to the vernacular may have been prompted in response to George Butterick's 1976 claim that for all of their virtues, Ferrini's poems "do not extend the limits of language or create an alternative world."[11]

The shift toward dialect proved gradual even within *Know Fish* itself. Book I of the epic, titled "The Lady of Misbegotten Voyages," begins in standardized English, and departures from that standard are few and far between. A triad of postscripts to one poem are labeled "PSa," "PPSa" and "PPSa" (20–21), suggesting vernacular formations to be jocular afterthoughts. A few pages later, Ferrini closes another poem with the hopeful injunction to "be who's you and the kids can be!" (25). But for the most part, the turn to Italian American dialect is deferred until "Da Songs," where Ferrini begins "replantin a rapscallion english" (152) in poem after poem.

Notably, "Da Songs" registers as a mischievous sequence not only on the strength of its rapscallion English, but also on the strength of its rapscallion Italian. Thus Ferrini renders the English "forget" as "faget" only after rendering the Italian "mangia" as "manja" (192–93). If there is a certain amount of mockery in such linguistic play, it also derives in

---

11 George F. Butterick, in the preface to Ferrini's *Selected Poems* ix. Having undertaken an extension of the limits of language, Ferrini's subsequent editors have been lukewarm toward such innovations. In *KF*, Book I, "Our Lady of the Misbegotten Voyages," unfolds across pp. 1–116 in standard English, while Book II, "Da Songs," proceeds via the vernacular across pp. 119–373. But in *WS*, although "Da Songs" is recognized as "an innovation in his work" (194), and although it is, in its original form, more than twice as long by page count, Ferrini's vernacular sequence is actually afforded fewer pages than the standard English sequence "Our Lady of the Misbegotten Voyages."

part from the concomitant mockery of American political economy, which Ferrini condenses to a pair of related principles: "Make tings t break down fast / n nothin t last," and "exploit n save / fa you grave" (141). The justice of such verdicts regarding the American system is underwritten here and elsewhere by a tenor of linguistic grotesquerie that runs throughout "Da Songs," bespeaking a larger trend within Italian American poetry toward what Martino Marazzi describes as "the fascination of verses that are irredeemably ugly."[12]

Without question, class-consciousness propels such modes of critique, but these forms of class-consciousness are inevitably inflected—if not defined—by questions of ethnicity. Contrasting the "fadda mudda son" with the "aristocrat ov gentility," Ferrini identified himself with the former category in a disarming self-portrait entitled "DA FAR IN FACE: Venanziano." Born Venanzio Ferrini, his first published poems appeared under the anglicized byline of Vincent Ferrous, and while this ironclad pseudonym was quickly discarded in favor of his actual family name, it took forty years and more for his actual given name to appear in print.[13] Positioned as a foreigner at the core of his identity, one whose very visage retained a remote aspect from first to last, Ferrini suggests himself in "DAR FAR IN FACE" as a figure whose marginalization is more than skin-deep and closely bound up in his liminality; poised between the hegemon and the subaltern, Venanziano stands

wit mind n tongue
between masta n slave-
n in da remoteness hearin
da slime
n da light slide (285)

As a destabilizing remainder astride the master-slave dialectic, attuned to both modalities but possessed of neither, Ferrini's identity politics are slippery indeed, and especially difficult to parse not only via conventional binary narratives of racial privilege and dispossession, but also via the usual complications thereof.

Although *Da Songs* can be read as a gesture of disaffiliation from an Italian or American (which is to say, a national) context, it can also be read as a gesture of affiliation within an Italian American (which is to say, an ethnic) context. More generally, the collective title *Know Fish*

---

[12]Marazzi 18. See also Vitiello, who speculates on this same aesthetic of ugliness (37).

[13]Noted by Butterick in his preface to Ferrini's *Selected Poems* xii. As Andrew Rolle has observed, "pressure to change family names by eliminating vowels or shortening them" (40) intensified in the lead-up to World War II, at the very moment when Ferrini first broke into print.

functions as a sort of imperative not only for the poem's readership, but also for Ferrini himself. Born in Saugus and raised in Lynn, Ferrini was nearly forty years old before relocating to Gloucester, and as a result, his knowledge of the fishing industry was rudimentary at first and remained cursory at best. Moreover, he was of a different regional line of descent than most of the other Italian Americans on Cape Ann, a fact that would have been reinforced at the annual St. Peter's Fiesta each June, which centered around a Sicilian American community with deep roots in Gloucester. Nevertheless, despite these regional distinctions, Ferrini's "Da Songs," like the St. Peter's Fiesta, functioned as a cultural practice announcing an ethnic departure from overarching societal norms, and as a symbolic monument to a more particularized mode of community identity.[14]

In view of this communitarian ethic, it's worth re-emphasizing that while many poets working in dialect forms have tended to apply distinct dialects to distinct speakers, or single dialects to many speakers of a single type, Ferrini assimilated all of the characters in Da Songs to the terms of his own Italian American vernacular. This vernacular was not reflective of a single regional dialect, but rather served as an invented amalgam indicative of nothing so much as Ferrini's own anxieties over the attenuation of his heritage. We might speak of Ferrini's dialect in *Know Fish* as Robert Viscusi has spoken of Pietro Di Donato's dialect in *Christ in Concrete* (1939), namely, as a language that is "the vehicle of the desire to remember," a language "never spoken by anyone except the American son of the lost Italian father" (100).[15]

Nevertheless, while Di Donato employed dialect forms in order to provide depth to a specific subset of the characters within the space of his narrative, the peculiar speaker of "Da Songs"—which is to say, the peculiar speech of "Da Songs"—speaks on behalf of every single Gloucester subject that appears in the sequence. Rather than enunciating a singular subjectivity or a fictive subjectivity, this speaker seems to exist in relatively close proximity to the author himself. Without question, Ferrini makes a point of self-identifying in "Da Songs" with a very specific strain of the people whom he labels "mustard / Ginnees" (159), and describes himself in rather particular terms as a "Moon goat frum da Mountains ov Abruzzi" (230). Nevertheless, when he addresses the reader as "paisan," there is also an ethnic detachment at work. On the one hand, Ferrini draws upon a crucial Italian American term of endearment, but on the

---

[14] For more on the St. Peter's Fiesta, see Swiderski.

[15] That said, Ferrini's work takes a much more skeptical approach to the reproduction of patriarchy; see, for example, his parodic take on the well-worn Mafia theme from "Da Songs," titled "DA GODMUDDA" (*KF* 299).

other hand, he applies this term to a highly dispersed and relatively diverse readership that is multiethnic and indeed transnational.[16]

Even as it suggested a fruitful avenue for future work in Italian American poetics, Ferrini's approach in "Da Songs" was an exceptional circumstance in his own career trajectory. In subsequent books of *Know Fish,* he reverted to standard English, and while in later efforts he returned to Italian American themes, he never returned to the vernacular as a means to that end.[17] Yet the exception of "Da Songs" is indicative of Ferrini's general ear for poetry, which was closely linked, as in the cases of Williams, Olson, and Baraka, to his ethnic estrangement from more standard forms of discourse within the American scene.[18]

As sociolinguist Michael Stubbs has explained, "transcribing conversation into the visual medium is a useful estrangement device," calling attention to "complex aspects of conversational coherence which pass us by as real-time conversationalists or observers" (20). It may well be that the complexities and idiosyncracies of Ferrini's cultural position enabled him to better appreciate and reproduce the complexities and idiosyncracies of the language as spoken by a particular population in a particular place and time. In this respect, it may be better to construe him as one of the first of the multiethnic "weird English" poets than to continue thinking of him as "the last surviving Proletarian Poet" of them all.

Finally, if "Da Songs" unfolds in a casual, offhanded manner, it must be remembered that its appearance in print came only after decades of experience, working strictly against the grain vis-à-vis stock-in-trade representations of Italian Americans, and succeeding only via sustained attention and dedication to the cultural heritage of an underrepresented population. As Ferrini explained to his protégé David Bianchini,

> ya gotta tunnel thru da repeating sham
> if ya gonna let ya origins jive
> zo kick da drug ov distrakshuns, man! (*KF* 328)

Beginning his career in the 1940s with a commitment to social realism, and transitioning in the 1950s and 1960s through a phase of more personal expression, Ferrini finally arrived, in "Da Songs," at a breakthrough

---

[16]"RAG PICCA: Trowaways"; in *KF* 182.

[17]Ferrini's epic continues in *Know Fish: Volume 2* (Book III, "The Navigators"); *Know Fish: Volume 3* (Book IV, "The Community of Self," and Book V, "The Illuminations"); and *Know Fish, Volume 4* (Book VI, "Shadows Talking," and Book VII, "This Other Ocean"). For Ferrini's later evocation of Italian American themes, see "Journey to Raiano," in *Magdalene Silences,* rep. in *WS* 147–51.

[18]For more on the specific parameters of the relationship between cultural estrangement and linguistic experimentation in an Italian American context, see Giunta.

synthesis of social and personal concerns. In channeling the social through the personal, Ferrini turned to a vernacular mode, working against those that he styled as the "robbas ov da sui generis" (248).[19]

But contrary to the extant Hollywood stereotypes, Ferrini was no robba. On the evidence of *Know Fish,* he was in fact a defender of "da sui generis." The robbas, for their part, have never really come to terms with what Ferrini got away with in "Da Songs."

Works Cited

Barolini, Helen, ed. *The Dream Book: An Anthology of Writings by Italian-American Women.* Rev. ed. Syracuse: Syracuse UP, 2000.

Biondi, Lawrence. *The Italian-American Child: His Sociolinguistic Acculturation.* Washington: Georgetown UP, 1975.

Butterick, George F., ed. *Charles Olson and Robert Creeley: The Complete Correspondence.* 9 vols. Santa Barbara: Black Sparrow P, 1980–1990.

___. "Vincent Ferrini." *American Poets, 1880–1945: Second Series.* Ed. Peter Quartermain. *Dictionary of Literary Biography* 48. Detroit: Gale Research, 1986.

Ch'ien, Evelyn Nien-Ming. *Weird English.* Cambridge: Harvard UP, 2005.

Cifelli, Edward M. *John Ciardi: A Biography.* Fayetteville: U of Arkansas P, 1997.

Clark, Tom. *Charles Olson: The Allegory of a Poet's Life.* New York: Norton, 1991.

Ferrini, Vincent. *Blood of the Tenement.* Lynn: Sandpiper, 1944.

___. *Hermit of the Clouds: The Autobiography of Vincent Ferrini.* Gloucester: Ten Pound Island Book, 1988.

___. *The Hiding One.* Brookline: Me and Thee P, 1973.

___. *I Have the World.* London: Fortune P, 1967.

___. *In The Arriving.* London: Heron P, 1954.

___. *The Infinite People.* New York: Great Concord, 1950.

___. *Injunction.* Lynn: Sandpiper, 1943.

___. *Know Fish: Volume 1* (Book I, "The Lady of Misbegotten Voyages," and Book II, "Da Songs"). Storrs: U of Connecticut Library, 1979.

___. *Know Fish: Volume 2* (Book III, "The Navigators"). Storrs: U of Connecticut Library, 1984.

___. *Know Fish: Volume 3* (Book IV, "The Community of Self," and Book V, "The Illuminations"). Storrs: U of Connecticut Library, 1986.

___. *Know Fish, Volume 4* (Book VI, "Shadows Talking," and Book VII, "This Other Ocean"). Storrs: U of Connecticut Library, 1991.

___. *Magdalene Silences.* Bedford, NH: Igneus P, 1992.

___. *No Smoke.* Portland, Maine: Falmouth Publishing House, 1943.

___. *Selected Poems.* Ed. George F. Butterick. Storrs: U of Connecticut Library, 1976.

---

[19] Ferrini would later explain to Peter Anastas, as subsequently quoted in Butterick's *DLB* entry, that his own poetry evolved over time from "the social" to "the personal" to "the social and personal together."

____. *Ten Pound Light.* Gloucester: Church P, 1975.

____. *Tidal Wave: Poems of the Great Strikes.* New York: Great Concord P, 1946.

____. *The Whole Song: Selected Poems.* Ed. Kenneth A. Warren and Fred White-
head. Urbana: U of Illinois P, 2004.

Giunta, Edvidge. *Writing With an Accent: Contemporary Italian American Women
Authors.* New York: Palgrave, 2002.

Marazzi, Martino, ed. *Voices of Italian America: A History of Early Italian American
Literature with a Critical Anthology.* Trans. Ann Goldstein. Madison, NJ: Farleigh Dickinson UP, 2004.

Masters, Edgar Lee. *Spoon River Anthology.* New York: Touchstone, 2004.

Miller, Wayne, ed. *Gathering of Ghetto Writers: Irish, Italian, Jewish, Black and
Puerto. Rican.* New York: New York UP, 1972.

Olson, Charles. *The Maximus Poems.* Ed. George F. Butterick. Berkeley: U of California P, 1983.

Rolle, Andrew. *The Italian Americans: Troubled Roots.* New York: Free P 1980.

Stubbs, Michael. *Discourse Analysis: The Sociolinguistic Analysis of Natural Language.* Chicago: U of Chicago P, 1983.

Swiderski, Richard M. *Voices: An Anthropologist's Dialogue with an Italian-American Festival.* Bowling Green, OH: Bowling Green State U Popular P, 1987.

Tallman, Warren. "Wonder Merchants: Modernist Poetry in Vancouver during the
1960's." *boundary* 2 3.1 (Autumn 1974): 57–90.

Tedesco, Jo Ann. "Sacraments: Italian American Theatrical Culture and the Drama-
tization of Everyday Life." *The Italian American Heritage: A Companion to Literature and Arts.* Ed. Pellegrino D'Acierno. New York: Garland, 1999. 353–86.

Viscusi, Robert. *Buried Caesars and Other Secrets of Italian American Writing.* Albany: SUNY P, 2006.

Vitiello, Justin. "Off the Boat and Up the Creek without a Paddle—or, Where Italian
Americana Might Swim: Prolepsis of an Ethnopoetics." *Beyond the Margin:
Readings in Italian Americana.* Ed. Paolo Giordano and Anthony Julian Tam-
burri. Madison, NJ: Farleigh Dickinson UP, 1998. 23–45.

Wheelwright, John. *Selected Poems.* Norfolk, CT: New Directions, 1941.

KATHLEEN MCCORMICK

CITY MOVES IN A "FEMININE KEY"

In this essay, I map the psychological terrain covered by three Italian American female figures—at three different life points and from three different texts—as they negotiate the cities in which they live. The characters are Anna Giardino in *Miss Giardino* by Dorothy Bryant, Gina in *The Right Thing to Do* by Josephine Gattuso Hendin, and Marianna DeMarco Torgovnick in her memoir *Crossing Ocean Parkway.* As these women leave their families for their city lives and interactions with others, their moves demonstrate the complex web of ethnicity, patriarchy, and social class that they each occupy. At every stage, they are met with contradictions that both inhibit their freedom of movement—psychological and physical—and simultaneously give them the strength to endure hostility and to embrace love, change, and development wherever they can find it.

Miss Giardino, by Dorothy Bryant, foregrounds issues of ethnic tension. Anna Giardino is near the end of her life. She doesn't move much geographically in the novel, but she is psychologically transported to different worlds as the immigrant populations of the San Francisco Mission District—where she was raised and teaches—shift around her. Further, her expectations of herself as a girl, woman, and retiree are challenged by racist, sexist, and ageist assumptions. *The Right Thing to Do,* by Josephine Hendin, is a coming-of-age novel. It most directly confronts the patriarchal assumptions underlying conventional Italian American culture. The young Gina, just beginning her adult life, can hardly move at all. But, unlike Anna Giardino, Gina's lack of movement is not out of choice. She is literally under the eye of her ailing but staunchly controlling father. *Crossing Ocean Parkway,* a memoir by Marianna DeMarco Torgovnick, focuses most explicitly on issues of social class. Torgovnick, who is in midlife, offers her readers a representation of movement within the city that might look seamless to an outside observer, but that is actually rife with contradiction and often pain. The tensions and dissonances within each of these texts in relation to ethnicity, patriarchy, and social class are particularly highlighted when juxtaposed to the others.

Unwitting Complicity of Fathers in Helping Daughters
Move Out of Conventional Roles

Being an Italian American female within the family structure represented in these books is largely inseparable from being a female in patriarchy, except that the fathers in each of these texts are unwittingly
complicit in their daughters' moving out of conventional roles. While this
kind of father-daughter relationship may not always be the norm in Italian American family structures, it is a story that is told repeatedly and
that bears significant notice, particularly in its subtle variations. I will
argue throughout this essay that it is neither the repression nor the support, but the interesting and contradictory combination of the two, that
encourages strength in the women depicted.

The fathers are represented in varying degrees as intentionally or
unintentionally destructive. Remembering her father on his deathbed,
Anna Giardino recalls her uneasiness at his weakness: "without his an-
chor, his fury, his cruelty, what is left?" And she asks herself "Where is
the man I hate?" (17). Fathers are depicted as literally wanting to control
their daughters' physical movements. Nino in *The Right Thing to Do* offers the most explicit representation of the controlling patriarch as he
actually follows Gina out of the house, into the subway, and around New
York. Fathers are also portrayed as denying and devaluing their daughters' intelligence. Torgovnick is pressured by her teachers and her parents to enter the secretarial track in high school, a route which was
common for Italian American girls, and she is reduced to making an em-
barrassing argument that plays upon her father's ethnic and class prejudice: "If I were Jewish I would have been placed, without question, in
the academic track." Torgovnick observes that: "In thinking about going
to college, I had convinced myself already that Italian Americans did not
value girls and especially girls who were good at the kinds of things I
liked—reading, thinking, and writing" (25). These feelings of being den-
igrated because one loves learning are shared by Anna, whose "father
calls her a dozen filthy names" (34) when she is accepted to college;
and by Gina, whose father taunts her: "I let you go to college . . . but do
you think you'll ever finish?" (59).

Yet each of the fathers has, seemingly unconsciously, given his daughter the very strength she needs to make her city moves. Anna describes
her father on his deathbed: "You know, he says, with just a shadow of the
old cruel irony, 'you . . . are like . . . me . . . or you could . . . never have
done it'" (17). His strength and determination have been passed down
to his daughter who, though demeaned by him, is also identified with him
on some level. Gina comments that she "suspected Nino wanted her to
succeed in college as much, maybe even more, than she did. He just
wouldn't admit it" (58). Comparable comments are repeatedly scattered
throughout the book: "She was his daughter; she was too much like him"
(58). Again, amid the repression, we see mutual identification. Perhaps

because it is a memoir rather than a novel, Torgovnick is more reflective about how feelings of patriarchal control can encourage a daughter to break with its very bonds; she remarks that "in retrospect this Italian devaluing of intelligence in girls seems not to have been entirely true," though she notes that it "hardly matters" because it was an "enabling fiction . . . I had many fantasies about life outside of Bensonhurst, in 'the city' . . . about upward mobility in a feminine key" (25) that this fiction helped sustain. Similar fantasies are shared by Gina and Anna.

But it is hardly the repression alone—fictive or real—that leads these girls to independence; rather, it is the contradictory nature of their relationships with the patriarchs of the family that enable them to put into reality the fantasy of those city moves in a feminine key. The father-daughter connections that prepare these women to make their moves in the world are complex and contradictory. The fathers are patriarchal and demean women, but they also admire and encourage an inner strength in their daughters.

City Moves: Agency in the World

That contradictory inner strength is reflected in these women's attitudes toward moving in the world: they evince a simultaneous sense of possibility and a strain of caution, holding each of them in some way to the past. The train into Manhattan serves as a means of escape for Gina throughout the novel. But looking at the Triborough Bridge, she thinks to herself that "if it seemed like a route to possibility, it also implied that some possibilities were out of reach" (31). Getting out of Bensonhurst for Torgovnick meant "freedom to experiment, to grow, to change" (10). Yet, like Gina, she openly acknowledges that some possibilities for change are out of reach: "You can take the girl out of Bensonhurst . . . but you may not be able to take Bensonhurst out of the girl" (10). Anna Giardino remembers the thrill of distancing herself from her family home as she applied for her first job: "This is the first time I have climbed west from Mission Street" (26). And yet as she observes, rather ironically, later in the book: "When I was a student, Mr. Robles told me to study and go to college or I'd never get out of the mission. But I never did get out, even though I did what he told me" (122). While these women feel empowered by identifying with the strength of their fathers, their ability to move out of their repressive pasts is also limited by their fathers' criticism and lack of faith in them.

Being an Italian Woman in the World: A Repetition of the Ambivalence in the Home

Let us turn at this point to the reception in the world with which these women are met as Italian Americans. We discover, once again, that for each of them, this reception is contradictory. As a young girl, Anna received encouragement from one of her high-school teachers, and, she discovers, after being mugged near the end of her life, that her career has been successful, that she was much more respected by her students than she had realized. However she has also experienced prejudice—in different forms—as the population of the Mission District shifted. When young, Anna was looked down upon by members of other white ethnicities because she was Italian (74); in later life, she is seen as racist because she is old and white and refuses to embrace black identity politics (63).

While Gina also meets with approval at school, she experiences repressive prejudice from her boyfriend, Alex, and his family. Ironically, while she is drawn to Alex because he is apparently so different from her father, Alex proves to be literally more predatory than Nino. From his biting her during sex to choosing the clothes she will wear during their visit to his parents, he and his family demean her because of her ethnicity and her social class. Alex's mother's eyes "raked her over, lingered on her face and hair, took in her clothes, recoiled from her shoes, and found the whole, Gina could see, unacceptable" (137). Marianna Torgovnick also experienced prejudice. In "a college town in New England" (59), she collided with " the College way" which expected "good fortune" from its citizens: her son became ill and eventually died in surgery, an unacceptable breach of propriety. Her ethnicity was also a continual irritant. From being told that she could visit a colleague only "if I promised not to cry" (65) because Italians are thought to be excessively emotional, to being "repeatedly mistaken . . . for a Jewish woman" whom she didn't resemble (69), she was aware that her ethnicity was on parade and a subject of ridicule.

Thus the mixed sense of confidence with which these Italian American women enter the world gets an equally mixed reception that provides painful echoes of the ambivalence of their fathers' reactions to them. Yet because they learned how to negotiate the undercutting and often negative response to them in their families, they are able to stay relatively strong in the face of prejudicial reaction to them in the outside world.

A Final Reaffirmation of Feminine Strength

I'd like to end with a key city scene from each book that reaffirms the ultimate strength of these women. The chase on which Gina takes Nino when she realizes that he is following her is in some ways a microcosm of the entirety of *The Right Thing to Do.* The decay of the Washington Square Park area in the book, the part of the city most laden with Nino's memories, mirrors the decay of his relationship with Gina and his own decaying gangrenous body. Yet we are not left solely with a sense of loss. The arguments Gina has with her father about her freedom and sexuality that follow from this scene lead to an unsentimentalized resolution between the dying Nino and Gina. Gina ends the novel recognizing the restlessness in herself that she inherited from her father: " 'Time,'

Gina thought, [the world] . . . 'looks like a train and I absolutely must get on'" (201).

In Bryant's *Miss Giardino,* the most intense city scene occurs in the layering of past and present that Anna Giardino experiences as she tries to recall the details of her mugging. Remembering her plan to burn down the school and the events surrounding her attempt starkly displays the "full force of her stored up anger" (145). Although she is near the end of her life, in contrast to Gina who is just beginning her adult life, both Anna and Gina are able to start anew. In selling her house and thinking about writing a book about the Mission District, she, like Gina, is embracing change, boarding the train, even if she gets off at the next stop.

The essential city move in *Crossing Ocean Parkway* is the change from literally making that crossing, to repeating it symbolically in the oscillation between memoir and cultural and literary criticism in the book itself. In this at times seamless, at other times more jarring, crossing between genres, Torgovnick's book elegantly uncoils, like Ocean Parkway, stretching and funneling the experiences of her life. Torgovnick is walking a path that crosses and recrosses Ocean Parkway, as Anna Giardino both literally and figuratively, in her memory after the mugging, rewalks the path between her house and her school. Torgovnick, like Giardino, discovers the capacity to change in crossing and recrossing this path. Gina, similarly, repeatedly rides the trains of New York in preparation for the rest of her life, for what she calls "the trip out" (35). Once you move out, Gina realizes, "you keep moving out. And it's not something you want to stop" (201).

For Gina, Anna Giardino, and for Torgovnick, because they are Italian, because they are women, because they are working class, there is no hope in the smug assurance that "nothing will change" (Torgovnick 62). Rather, the hope is that change, however plodding, however embedded in the past, is always possible, and that women who have been oppressed at home and in the larger world—regardless of age—can move within the contradictions of that oppression, using it against itself to cross in a "feminine key" to new and transformative paths.

Works Cited

Bryant, Dorothy. *Miss Giardino: A Novel.* Berkeley: Ata Books, 1978.

Hendin, Josephine. *The Right Thing to Do.* Boston: Godine, 1988.

Torgovnick, Marianna. *Crossing Ocean Parkway.* Chicago: U of Chicago P, 1996.

TRACY FLOREANI

THE VERY STRANG TRUTH
Ben Piazza's Italian Southerner

While "whiteness studies" in the late 1990s saw its star rise and fall pretty quickly, its renewed examination of social constructions of race benefited ethnic studies in highlighting a persistent and crucial line of inquiry: namely, how have immigrants and ethnic Americans positioned themselves within the racial divide at various historical moments? Locating and examining this positioning in various texts helps to deepen the study of ethnicity as a nonstatic cultural category throughout the country's history.

Ben Piazza's 1964 novel *The Exact and Very Strange Truth* serves as a particularly fruitful site for investigating the positioning of Italian American identity within the middle decades of the twentieth century. Though Piazza's novel is not widely known, it makes a significant contribution to the increasingly important body of work by ethnic writers of the post-World War II era because of the ways in which it questions identity categories and exposes some of the cultural mechanisms of identity construction specific to the postwar United States. His novel offers an intriguing negotiation of racial lines in a setting not typical for Italian American artists, the American South. However, the region serves as more than a backdrop upon which to investigate his character's "hybrid" identity. Piazza's narrative relies on elements of the estranged and bizarre, like those that typify the writings of such contemporaries as Carson McCullers and Flannery O'Connor, to effectively disrupt the typically white genre of the "Southern grotesque."

The story takes place in the 1940s, covering a span of years roughly coinciding with World War II. The narrative begins with twelve-year-old Alexander Gallanti accompanying his mother, who is suffering the aftermath of a stroke, and two younger siblings, Veronica and Quentin, on a plane trip from Little Rock, Arkansas, to Savannah, Georgia, so that their mother can recuperate near the ocean and her oldest son Rudolph. The trip serves as a framework for the novel, with Alexander offering his family's story as the bulk of the narrative, apparently occupying the duration of the nighttime flight during which the adolescent cannot sleep. Piazza's use of free indirect discourse allows him to slip into and out of Alexander's voice for whole sections of the book, to offer a narrative that goes beyond the temporal parameters of the flight. Consequently, we learn (nonchronologically) about the parents' courtship, the father's immigration and experiences with discrimination, the lives of Alexander's many siblings, and their father's death. In all of this, the narrative consistently returns to Alexander's nagging sense of isolation within his large family, and to his attempts to connect with various nonfamilial figures throughout his childhood, from African American domestic workers to a sleeping couple he watches through a window every morning on his paper route.

In addition to the classic "grotesque" elements that pepper the book, such as a lengthy description of a freak show; a story about a baby who gets his arm gnawed off by a giant rat; and Alexander's gift of nicely wrapped chicken heads for a sister-in-law he hates, the novel relies on the subtler thematic grotesque that has become a trademark of much twentieth-century Southern literature. Alexander Gallanti is consistent with Alan Spiegel's now well-known exploration of the grotesque Southern character, whose physical or psychological "deformity" renders him an outcast (429). In this, the grotesque Southern character reads as an exaggerated version of the archetypal alienated modern, one whose story often takes place among other social misfits or against a backdrop of the bizarre.

Piazza's reliance on this Southern mode is so strong that the voice in his novel at times seems to read as an Italianized version of Carson McCullers's *The Member of the Wedding.* In a manner resembling McCullers's tomboyish Frankie, the somewhat effeminate Alexander of Piazza's novel spends much of his time with black female domestic workers and develops ambivalent relations with them as surrogate parental figures. Socially rejected and isolated, both protagonists also make notably awkward attempts at sexual experience. Their physical features (Frankie's excessive height and boyish behavior, Alexander's blond hair and blue eyes) define them and cause them to be afraid of other social misfits. In order to highlight how deeply these characters fear they are at the threshold of complete rejection, each story emphasizes a visit to a carnival freak show. Alexander feels drawn to Miss Minus and The Asian Duck Lady, yet he simultaneously fears he may someday become a "freak" too (116). In McCullers's story, Frankie experiences something similar: ". . . it seemed to her that they had looked at her in a secret way and tried to connect their eyes with hers, as though to say: we know you" (272).

Both characters also seek to mitigate their feelings of isolation from their families and peers by inventing a revised familial unit that presumes a psychic connection with others who are ignorant of the protagonists' desires. Frankie plans to run away to Alaska with her older brother and his new wife, expecting to be accepted automatically as a third member of the marriage. Her conceptualization of this three-way relationship is amorphous, since we do not know whether she is seeking parental figures or acting upon romantic jealousy. She sees the connection with the young couple simply as an extension of self, what she calls "the we of me" (291). Alexander parallels this kind of desire at two places in Piazza's book: early in his childhood when he imagines himself as the "third twin" to a set of twins he admires at school, and, later, in what he calls "the secret place of us" that he hopes to discover when the quartet of family members arrives at their new home in Savannah. I draw these comparisons not just to underscore how much Piazza's narrative shares with McCullers's, but to demonstrate how immersed in the modernist Southern grotesque Piazza's novel is, and how the voice of Alexander can ultimately be read as both Italian and modern Southern.

Through this stylistic mode, combined with racialized cultural commentary like that found in the works of Southern writers such as Lillian Smith and Harper Lee, Piazza calls into question the practices that influence and maintain notions of identity within American culture. As the child of a Sicilian father and a Southern Baptist mother, the boy Alexander is socially isolated because he fits no clear category. He is marked by his Italianness because of his father's stereotypical Sicilian physical features and unabashed performance as cultural Other (as, for example, when he spends Sundays touring Little Rock in a small convertible sports car and drinking wine). In the segregated South, the presence of his father's Italian cobbler shop within Little Rock's white commercial district confuses the social order, so much so that the Ku Klux Klan and other white citizens' groups who see the family as racially Other try to scare him into leaving. On the other hand, Alexander is simultaneously marked by his "blue eyes and cotton hair" in a way that calls into question the "authenticity" of his Italianness, both for his siblings, who teasingly accuse him of not being their father's child, and for other members of Little Rock's white community, who expect him to be stereotypically dark in coloring—even as they address him with derogatory ethnic names. At one point, in an effort to look more like his dark-haired siblings, Alexander attempts to dye his hair with black ink, which turns half of his face and half of his hair an unnatural black (28). Here and in many parts of the novel, Alexander's hybridity is played out in the symbolic. For example, he receives a mark of "unsatisfactory" in citizenship (10), but also spends several days dressed as a pilgrim, chanting to himself "I am a Pilgrim. I am a Pilgrim" (249). Ultimately, Alexander fails in his attempts to embody any one paradigm. The black ink is not permanent, and the virtuous American Pilgrim costume is only a costume. Those around him see him as a strange kid who will not take off his Thanksgiving pageant outfit, and as an "unfit" Italian whose identity is called into question because his physiognomy and ethnicity render him incomprehensible in a context that requires certainty in all matters of identity.

Rose Basile Green, one of the few critics to have written about Piazza's novel, focuses her analysis on the theme of the inevitability of change. As Piazza's child narrator Alexander explains the book's title, "Things change so sudden sometimes and that is the exact and very strange truth. Always and forever things change" (326). Basile Green reads this theme as a metaphor for the larger cultural changes taking place within the South of the 1960s, arguing that the story is largely about race relations and how "attitudes toward these relations are changing" (225). She argues further that "Piazza emphasizes the cultural tradition of the Italian-American by juxtaposing it to the unidentifiable morass that the Negroes were once forced to inhabit in the traditional South" (227–28). To support this interpretation, she cites examples of the Italian American characters forging relationships with the minor African American characters, such as when Alexander's father demands that a white hospital treat his black housekeeper's baby, the one whose arm has been gnawed off by the giant rat. Through such examples, Basile Green suggests that the newer Italian immigrants occupy a similar cultural space to that inhabited by pre-Civil Rights-era African Americans.

Documented discrimination against Italian immigrants includes Reconstruction policies that kept Italians out of Southern states (especially South Carolina), and the lynching of eleven Italian workers in New Orleans in 1891. David A. J. Richards also notes that nineteenth-century Italian immigrants arrived "in the midst of a revolutionary struggle over the meaning of nationalism," resulting in forms of discrimination against Italians that qualify as what he terms "moral slavery" (3–5). Paralleling Italian experiences in the U.S. with those of African Americans does have its limits, however. While Italians were originally seen as a different "race" when they arrived in the United States, they did arrive within a historical context in which the horrors of slavery could not have been enacted upon them to the same extent because they were never legally regarded as property. While they were actively and sometimes violently discriminated against, their bodies were not categorically and systematically objectified and exploited in the way that those of nineteenth-century African Americans had been.

Furthermore, during World War II, Italian American men participated as whites within the segregated military, which allowed them to transform their cultural positions and to escape the category of race. Richards describes the darker side of this assimilative process as a reactive suppression of cultural identities within a nativist culture. Specifically in the 1940s, Lawrence Distasi demonstrates in *Una Storia Segreta: The Secret History of Italian American Evacuation and Interment During World War II* how, like Japanese Americans, Italians on the American home front self-censured as a reaction to nationally condoned discrimination against

Italian Americans because of an implied connection to fascism. Regardless, after the war Italian Americans were afforded the housing and employment opportunities that came with the privilege of whiteness. Humbert S. Nelli documents how Italians (like American Jews) partook of the educational opportunities provided by the G.I. Bill and participated in the reconfiguration of American residential spaces with the help of monies provided by the Veterans Administration and the Federal Housing Authority. FHA policies (in place until the mid–1960s) stipulated that monies be invested only in new housing and development, not in the purchase and renovation of existing structures in the urban core. These policies were specifically in place to avoid funding homes in areas with the potential for "inharmonious racial or national groups" (Nelli 173–74). Consequently, Little Italies dwindled as younger generations with new families moved out to suburbs.

Other postwar cultural historians have noted how both government policies regarding American families as well as media representations of family encouraged and reinforced patterns in which "the isolated nuclear family and its concerns eclipsed previous ethnic, class, and political forces as the crucible of personal identity" (Lipsitz 55). With this reconfiguration of the idea of family came a shift in the perception of second-generation immigrants. The attitudes Karen Brodkin Sacks documents in her study of postwar Jewish whiteness applies to many immigrant groups: "[s]uddenly the same folks who promoted nativism and xenophobia were eager to believe that Euro-origin people whom they had deported, reviled as members of inferior races, and prevented from immigrating only a few years earlier were now model middle-class white suburban citizens" (79). By the 1960s the label "Italian" had morphed from a separate racial designation into a somewhat popularly marketable form of "ethnic," a set of "exotic" cultural features possessed by midcentury icons such as Frank Sinatra, Tony Bennett, Mario Lanza, Louis Prima, and Sofia Loren. While Basile Green suggests that the Italian American family is naturally allied with African American characters, Alexander's emotional confusion demonstrates that he is much less certain of any ally, as his family is in the middle of a complicated cultural repositioning.

The various generations of the Gallanti family in Piazza's novel act out the social shift, with the father representing the racialized first generation, his oldest sons beginning the shift toward whiteness through their military service and participation in the postwar economy, and his youngest children left with the promise of unquestioned whiteness by the time they become adults. Alexander's older brother Rudolph, having served with the American forces during the war, moves to Savannah with his Jewish American bride to establish a cobbler shop. His shop reads as a metaphorical restructuring of the postwar ethnic: The façade is a perfect facsimile of his father's store, but the inside is completely modernized and unrecognizable to Alexander as the shop in which all of them grew up working (292). Moreover, Rudolph and Miriam symbolically enact Southern whiteness as they take the visiting family members on a day–long tour of Confederate monuments. By the end of the novel, Alexander has not attempted an active embrace of Southern whiteness to the same extent that his older brother has, but the lack of a nuclear family—due to his father's death and his mother's stroke—certainly leaves him groundless in his identity. Such ambivalence on Alexander's part implies that racial and ethnic identities are neither a matter of choice nor a matter defined entirely by external factors.

After much family drama, the climactic scene in Savannah is hilariously classic Southern macabre and brings the theme of racial identity—and uncertainty—back to the foreground. While Rudolph and Miriam are off at work, the children are left alone to care for their mother. Since it is Alexander's thirteenth birthday, he decides they will dress up their mother and take her into town for a matinee of a revival showing of *Gone with the Wind.* In her mostly paralyzed state the mother does little to resist her children's attempts to do her makeup, so she ends up in garish clown-face with childish bows in her hair. Because she is unable to walk, the children have to transport her to the bus stop in a Radio Flyer wagon. After missing the bus, they hitch a ride into town with a black farmer in a horse cart. This is the seemingly antebellum conveyance with which the now paralytic Southern belle reaches the theater, Alexander waving and pretending he is in a special birthday parade all the while.

Before going to the cinema, Alexander attempts to explain the film to his younger brother in a conversation that indicates the disconnection of these children from white Southern identity. Piazza seems to use *Gone with the Wind* here intentionally, knowing that it serves as a cinematic anthem for this generation of white Southerners in its romantic evocation of the traditional South. Yet Alexander and his brother find it incomprehensible:

> Quentin said, "What movie are we going to see?'
> "*Gone with the Wind.*"
> "Gone where with the wind?"
> "I don't know, Quentin, gone wherever the wind went."
> "*What* is gone with the wind?" (306)

Donnalee Frega and Brigette Craft argue that many Southern writers found in the grotesque mode "a unique vehicle to express their sense of the absurdity of the [postwar] world . . ." (105). Piazza's use of the film falls in with other postwar Southern writers' attempts to reconcile the incompatibilities of the Old and New South. "Their glance is outward, not backward" as they offer commentary on what they observe "as they leave the safe repository of their regional past" (Frega and Craft 105). Now lacking connection to the Sicilian half of his identity because his father is dead, the narrative structure implies that Alexander should identify with the remaining Southern Baptist half of his family, symbolized by his participating in the audience's reverential viewing of *Gone with the Wind.*

To further complicate matters, however, the mother dies while in the movie theater, and the children are left as orphans with no "safe repository" for their cultural identities other than the mythic representation of Southernness on film. The children sit surrounded by an audience of Southern strangers. Here, the narrative voice suddenly shifts to an omniscient representation of the film's reception:

> They saw the images which they had had in their minds, the images of the Old South, come to life—the beautiful plantation homes with the high columns, the graceful Southern belles in hoop skirts, the Southern gentlemen talking of honor, the faithful and loving slaves and the many other myths in which they believed. (318)

Afterwards Veronica swoons, "'It wasn't like a movie, it was like it was real'" (319). Perhaps, unlike Alexander caught in the middle of the binary, his young sister is ready to inherit Southern whiteness. Yet Scarlett O'Hara's cinematic presence underlines the mythic nature of a pure white Southern identity.

Piazza cleverly stages Alexander's family life in the symbolic, in a world where identifiers are played with and provoked in order to expose how cultural identities are played out within the imaginary. Paradoxically, at the same time that the narrative questions the sanctity of Southern whiteness—and effectively disrupts the black/white binary that continues to define Southern literary studies by wedging ethnicity between the racial categories—*The Exact and Very Strange Truth* stylistically serves to reify Southern literature as a recognizable genre unto itself. On the surface, Alexander is unwilling to connect with his Southern relatives, as demonstrated in a scene where, in response to a relative's anti-integration sentiments, he spells out "F-A-T L-A-D-Y, Y-O-U D-O-N-T K-N-O-W A-N-Y-T-H-I-N-G" (261–62). In the end, however, Alexander is more like Frankie in *The Member of the Wedding* than he is like any of the black characters with whom he seeks to connect. The novel asserts what is essentially a white narrative, in which black characters make themselves available to a lonely and lost child, whose own struggle for self-definition ultimately leaves the black maternal figures behind. For Alexander, race and ethnicity turn out to be relatively ephemeral. Though attitudes about race, as Basile Green argues, may have been changing, race will never be ephemeral in the American South. As Alexander describes his imaginative sense of identity early in the book, "Sometimes I am whatever is where I am. In school sometimes I say to myself: I am school, I am desk, I am book. . . . *I am Christmas*" (104). The novel stops just short of suggesting that Alexander eventually may follow his little sister's lead and say, "I am *Gone with the Wind.*"

Works Cited

Distasi, Lawrence. *Una Storia Segreta: The Secret History of Italian American Evacuation and Interment During World War II.* Berkeley, CA: Heyday, 2001.

Frega, Donnalee, and Brigette Craft. "Disabling History: Contemporary Southern Literature's Solution." *Southern Literary Journal* 29.2 (1997): 103–21.

Green, Rose Basile. *The Italian-American Novel: A Document of the Interaction of Two Cultures.* Cranbury, NJ: Farleigh Dickinson UP, 1974.

Lipsitz, George. *Time Passages: Collective Memory and the American Popular Culture.* Minneapolis: U Minnesota P, 1990.

McCullers, Carson. *The Member of the Wedding.* 1946. Rpt. *Collected Stories.* Boston: Houghton Mifflin, 1987. 257–392.

Nelli, Humbert S. *From Immigrants to Ethnics: The Italian Americans.* New York: Oxford UP, 1983.

Piazza, Ben. *The Exact and Very Strange Truth.* New York: Farrar Straus, 1964.

Richards, David A. J. *Italian American: The Racializing of an Ethnic Identity.* New York: New York UP, 1999.

Sacks, Karen Brodkin. "How Did Jews Become White Folks?" *Race.* Ed. Steven Gregory and Roger Sanjek. New Brunswick, NJ: Rutgers UP, 1994. 78–102.

Spiegel, Alan. "A Theory of the Grotesque in Southern Fiction." *Georgia Review* 26 (1972): 426–37.

JOHN DOMINI

SKIRTS AND SLACKS, BROTHER FIRE
W.S. Di Piero Replaces "Hood with Word"

It's not as if, in his work before 2001, the sensual yet deeply meditative poet and essayist W. S. Di Piero had never written about South Philly. After all, by the turn of the current millennium this Stanford professor and contributing editor to *Threepenny Review* had six books of poetry and three collections of criticism and personal essays, in addition to award-winning translations from Italian and ancient Greek. Certainly the early poems of *The Only Dangerous Thing* (1984) addressed cultural transplantation, and the immigrant agony of his parents' generation. More pertinent to the explorations of this essay, in *Shooting the Works,* his 1996 collection of essays, reviews, and journal entries, there appear two *ars poetica* pieces, "Pocketbook and Sauerkraut" and "Gots Is What You Got," essays that locate determining factors for his art in the streets and the kitchens where he was raised.

Di Piero is a war child, born in 1945, and in "Pocketbook . . ." he relates how he grew up near Watkins and 21st, where the Italian-American working poor of Philadelphia were separated by a single block from African Americans no better off. Swiftly the essay gets into the tensions of that juxtaposition, classic tensions for urban America in the middle of the previous century:

> The black working people . . . though physically closer to us than any other group, in language . . . were demonized and made the most remote and adversarial. Ethnic and racial tags made up our richest vocabulary.

As for "Gots Is What You Got," the title derives from roughly the same vocabulary, an Italian obscenity garbled by the American-born generation; a fitting translation would be "you got dick." In this essay, Di Piero confesses that the interior language on which he draws for poetry "never did shed [its] tribal legacy of contrariness, . . . festive abrasiveness and chafing hilarity. . . ."

But in the years since that essay, that legacy has served this author better still. Two of Di Piero's recent collections, *Skirts and Slacks* from 2001 and *Brother Fire* 2005, both have major sequences set in South Philly, the opening third of *Skirts* and the closing third of *Brother,* and together these sequences notch a new benchmark for the poetry of urban, ethnic America. This essay will first comment on these poems generally, their linked subject matter and their manifold strengths, and afterward I'll detail one telling resource for them, namely, the way their "tribal contrariness" depends on a more or less African-American Other. If Di Piero has broken through to a new level of power, in what could've been a mere sentimental journey, part of the reason is the close presence of something shadowy, carnal, and violent, looming close enough to make every epiphany more nervous and humane. This presence is often expressed via signifiers for African-American city culture, which Di Piero skillfully manipulates, as a source of strength for his language and imagery. When he works in what we might call ghetto slang, colloquialisms associated with urban African-America, he accords it the respect of careful placement, at key junctures.

Overall, in these two sequences, the poet returns to his home ground with a vengeance, and that last word is no figure of speech. This is writing that calls to mind Edmund Wilson's "incurable wound," eternally bleeding. The opener in *Skirts and Slacks* ("'Philly Babylon,'" the first half of "Cheap Gold Flats") visits his mother's deathbed and, though it concludes with the words "forgive me," pulls off a half-drunken skewing of the expression. Then toward the end of *Brother Fire* the poet recalls saying his Hail Marys down on his knees beside that mother, as she stood ironing in their rowhouse basement; lines alternate between frustration over a "deity of hurt and rue" and sympathy for a parent who, he comes to feel, is as humble as he ("Prayer Meeting").

Di Piero fits this self-exposure into flexible form. Line-length serves as a defining factor for each piece, but runs shorter in one, longer in another. The poet mixes his pacing only in the longest poems, for instance during his attempt to revisit the local library in "The Apples" (in *Skirts*), and here the staggered lengths suit the poet's rediscovery of our transitory nature. City budget cuts have hacked away at the timeless dimension of words, and the library entrance is blocked by a cawing baglady.

While that poem's intimations of mortality emerge in stanzas of nine lines, a number of powerful pieces present a single unbroken utterance, like "Ortlieb's Uptown Taproom" (in *Fire*) which pits a brewery worker's routine against an imagined carefree Beyond, by means of a roadhouse band and the worker's recollection of Christmas-morning bagpipes back in his Italian home village. Other South-Philly meditations take shape in stanzas of three, four, or five lines, and stresses fall now three per line, now four. Both "'Philly Babylon'" and "Prayer Meeting" offer a jazzy American variation on blank verse.

This balance of formal concern, showing coherence within individual pieces and freedom across the sequence, contributes significantly to Di Piero's suppression of cliché, his refusal to gloss over either recollection or the experience on returning. But an emotional honesty that can induce shivers depends primarily, of course, on language. In the South Philly poems Di Piero's technique rises to levels of a tour de force which nonetheless never lack for a common touch; this paradox functions best through his artful use of active verbs. In "Gots Is What You Got," the poet makes special mention of verbs, when dissecting what he picked up from the talk across the stoops and countertops of his childhood: "tenses mix," he writes, "coalesce, bang, and sag."

And in a piece from *Skirts* which I'll consider more closely in a minute, "Leaving Bartram's Garden in Southwest Philadelphia," the poet first notes how "new-style trolleys squeak down Woodland," they ride on tires now rather than rails, and a few lines later he recalls what he glimpsed at one of the windows in the home of the Quaker botanist: "A redbird gashed the sunned mullioned glass." Then towards the poem's end, as his trolley moves through the dicey neighborhood close to the park, he doesn't miss how "[t]he brown-brick project softens in the sun," and "[t]agger signatures surf red and black / across the wall." Di Piero's craft likewise trolleys; it sways and rumbles, the better to illuminate "whatever is authentic," as he says in the "Gots" essay, and the authentic itself dwells in a "commingling of abstract . . . formal beauty with the given language textures . . . of my culture." When that commingling comes off, cultural referents from Dante to disco can all seem entirely apropos to a troubled ethnic enclave perceived with both a gimlet-eyed irony and, as in "Bartram's Garden," newly-forged awe at the oneness that embraces plant life, bird life, public transportation, and the art of the streets.

I suppose I should add that discerning critics have had high praise for these two books, notably Philip Levine in *Ploughshares* and Albert Mobilio in the *New York Times Book Review.* Their encomiums echo my own: Levine declares the poems have "the texture of American cities," and Mobilio says they set "dazzling moments amid plainsong."

That last referent I mentioned, the graffiti, means that this "Garden" ends in the ghetto. Transcendent connectedness here arrives prompted by homeboys, perhaps gangbangers:

Tagger signatures surf red and black

across the wall, fearless, dense lines
that conch and muscle so intimately
I can't tell one name from the other.

A poem that begins in a home that dates from slave times concludes with a distinctively cross-cultural, cross-racial re-imaging of the bird at the Quaker's window (and with one more flourish of verbs, "conch and muscle"). The feeling asserted earlier as a stray thought, "*I'm in the weave,*" is at climax embodied thanks to quasi-criminal urban youth. Precisely the sort of youth — need we even say youth of color? — whose image has been so often distorted by the national media into something thuggish and primitive. A talent like Di Piero however, fully mature, fully informed, inverts this signifier for the Other so that it expresses a concept quite the opposite, namely, the Universal.

The device, to be sure, performs a traditional function of poetry, locating the intangible in the down to earth. But when the grown Di Piero children converse across their mother's corpse in "Finished Basement," the latter half of "Cheap Gold Flats," that function is allied with rhythm and blues. The piece ends with Mom's presence made eerily tangible, fingering the poet's neck, but at the beginning a very different sensation emerged from the walls behind him: "Disco tracks / jump inside the paneling." A few lines further on, when the poem turns more directly to the deceased, it first sharply summarizes the children's conversation with two words: "Yackety-yak." A song by The Coasters, a crossover hit, takes our narrator from chattering denial to a chill sensation of the unknowable.

The first piece in the *Brother Fire* sequence, "Ortlieb's," also depends on black-music signifiers. Tonight the taproom features a sax player in a Hawaiian shirt and "porkpie," the onstage gear of Charles Mingus and many another jazzman. When the immigrant laborer who enjoyed the show later recalls the bagpipes of his mountain home, he hears their "goatskin bags call like animals," dark and atavistic, "like our flamingo sax, in his ecstasy tonight." One could say that this piece expounds on a folk-cultural manifestation of the genetic link between Africa and Southern Italy; in the "Gots" essay, we learn that Di Piero's mother came from Naples and his father from the Abruzzo. But then again, like any poem, this one has more to do with ecstasy than with sociology.

"Prayer Meeting," later in *Fire,* seems to eschew any such urban black signifiers — until one looks again at the very title and subject. An overworked mother and her child call on their Lord, together, aloud, one knocked to his knees by the Spirit and both half-mumbling, half-singing as "God jerked alive / in repetitions." As Di Piero evokes the setting, at the poem's close, it can't help but recall the furnishings in any neighborhood of outsiders and menials; mother and son pray under "splintered rafters weeping / wan work dungarees. . . ."

Another piece in the second book, "Lightning Bugs," constructs a metaphor that's hardly original; the easily trapped insects stand for our inextinguishable desires (desire imbues all *Brother Fire*; the book adapts this larger metaphor from a canticle of St. Francis). What saves the poem from sounding hackneyed, then, if not the sharp voice of what sounds an awful lot like a working class (African-American included) mom, calling down the block at twilight? "*Jo-Jo, / where you? Time to eat.*" At the end, bug and poet come together as a lurking B-&-E man, as he imagines the creature "a sensor house-light's // weegee when I pass. . . ."

The last poem in *Fire,* the last in both Philadelphia sequences, presents a portrait of the artist as a young Civil Rights sympathizer. "The Kiss" (which appeared in *The New Yorker*) recalls a preadolescent visit to Father Feeney. The priest calls the boy "my dear" and awards him a kiss, on the cheek but nevertheless uncalled for, while at the same time briskly disabusing his young charge of his desire to join the clergy. Thereafter, amid the subway's "Golgotha air of piss and smoke" — the adult poet, clearly, still wonders about the Father's steaming crotch — the youngster sees in the evening papers "black people / hosed down by cops or stretched by dogs," and at once he asks himself again the question asked some minutes before by his priest: "What was I running from?" So the fearsome shadow-self is suggested by the Father but witnessed, this night, in pictures of the people who Di Piero's neighbors demonized worst, and this carries the poet to his true calling, here as in an earlier poem made manifest on the surfaces of the city:

> . . . I believed the wall's
> filthy cracks, coming into focus
> when we stopped, held stories I'd find
> and tell.

Like Stephen Dedalus before him, the Di Piero of the South-Philly sequences has heard God in a shout in the street. This shout may take visual form, like a tagger's scrawl or, in the first stanza of "The Kiss," "summer hammerheads / whomping fireplugs." Nonetheless it's an outcry from the inner city, the black inner city. The loss of his parents may have gotten him into these poems, these visions, but in a number of cases, what gives them meaning and power comes from the people his parents warned him against.

Works Cited

Di Piero, W.S. *Brother Fire.* New York: Knopf, 2004.

____. *Chinese Apples: New and Selected Poems.* New York: Knopf, 2007.

____. *The Only Dangerous Thing.* Chicago, IL: Elpenor Books, 1984.

____. *Shooting the Works: On Poetry and Pictures.* Evanston, IL: TriQuarterly Books, Northwestern UP, 1996.

____. *Skirts and Slacks.* New York: Knopf, 2001.

Levine, Philip. "Bookshelf: Review of *Skirts and Slacks.*" *Ploughshares* 27.2–3 (2001): 275.

Mobilio, Albert. "Poems around the House: Review of *Skirts and Slacks.*" *New York Times Book Review* 5 Aug. 2001: 15.

Wilson, Edmund. *The Wound and the Bow.* Boston: Houghton Mifflin, 1941.

NANCY CARONIA

MEETING AT BRUCE'S PLACE
Springsteen's Italian American Heritage and Global Notions of Family

My soul is lost, my friend
Tell me how do I begin again?
My city's in ruins
—from Bruce Springsteen's
"My City of Ruins"

On the television screen only the Statue of Liberty and a tugboat sailing past the recently metamorphosed Manhattan skyline are lit. The view changes quickly to a stripped-down television studio illuminated by hundreds of white candles and a soft violet glow. Silhouettes, which become visible against the studio backdrop, create the appearance of a choir and a priest. From the shadows emanate the sounds of a harmonica and an acoustic guitar. As the studio lights come up, the harmonica is silenced and the priest-like figure murmurs, "This is a prayer for our fallen brothers and sisters" (*America: A Tribute to Heroes*). The camera focuses on the suddenly illuminated face of this man—a face that has graced a dozen album covers as well as magazine covers from *Time* to *Rolling Stone*. This is no priest; it is Bruce Springsteen.

On September 21, 2001, the Italian, Irish, and Dutch American rock and roller opened the *America: A Tribute to Heroes* benefit concert, which was broadcast globally to raise money for those affected by the September 11, 2001 attacks.[1] While Springsteen's live performances are

---

[1] Springsteen's father was of Dutch and Irish descent, while his mother Adele's grandmother, Raffaela Zerilli, arrived on Ellis Island on October 3, 1900. In 2010, Springsteen received an Ellis Island Family Heritage Award, presented to immigrants or their descendents who are deemed significant contributors to America.

regaled for their rock and roll spectacle, even "the Boss" could not easily fashion an adequate response to the devastation of those attacks: commercial airliners rammed into the Twin Towers and the Towers' subsequent collapse. To return order after the transpired chaos, Springsteen used his gifts of oratory and showmanship to build on what critic Robert Viscusi refers to as a "visionary political tradition" manifested in the skillful rhetoric of other Italian American public figures, such as former New York governor Mario Cuomo (130). Viscusi contends that this tradition, which he traces back to the Roman empire, is a periphrastic act that emphasizes the family as part of a larger community and that has been used to break an isolationist pattern found within the immigrant Italian American narrative. Viscusi further suggests that this practice opens up a space with "many U.S. political audiences who regarded the family as the first battleground of civic politics" (130–31). Springsteen has likely also drawn on Italian American notions of family learned from his mother, Adele, as he continues to integrate a sense of familial, moral, and civic responsibility in shaping his iconic rock and roll career. While his concerts are routinely praised for their sense of intimacy, they also, for example, regularly welcome donations for local food banks. Springsteen's related public advocacy work includes yearly December holiday shows to support the community of Asbury Park, New Jersey, touring for Amnesty International in 1988, and campaigning against California's Proposition 209 with California State Representatives in 1996. His civic commitment made him the ideal individual to set the tone for this benefit concert during an especially emotional and overwrought time in American political and cultural life.

On September 21, 2001, Springsteen called those who had lost their lives on 9/11 "our fallen brothers and sisters." This intimate gesture of familial solidarity connected a global television-viewing public to the catastrophic events in New York, Washington D.C., and Pennsylvania. In the five-minute-long performance, Springsteen recontextualized and rearranged "My City of Ruins," a song originally written for Asbury Park, a town on the New Jersey shore caught in a spiral of economic downturn and urban decay, into a hymn meant for a private ritual. The solemn and austere studio setup denoted the space as sacred and pointed out that the performance would not be a typical Springsteen rock and roll extravaganza. There were no shouts of "Bruuuuuuce!" No Clarence Clemons wailing on the saxophone or Max Weinberg pounding out the beat of a rock and roll anthem on his drums. Only his wife, the Italian American Patti Scialfa, and his childhood friend Steve Van Zandt sang backup alongside five additional anonymous members of the chorus.

"There's a blood red circle / On the cold dark ground," began Springsteen's hushed and reverent musical invocation, which elevated the televised benefit concert from what could have been a kitschy telethon to a globally broadcast memorial service for those lost on September 11 ("My

City of Ruins"). Those opening lines are metaphoric but clearly evoke the image of downtown Manhattan after the Towers' collapse, the space sometimes denoted as Ground Zero. By the time Springsteen uttered those words, most people understood that no more survivors would emerge from the rubble. Even remains were difficult to come by—human beings had been reduced to ash, which the city's population breathed in as the wind swirled memory of the sentient and nonsentient uptown to the West and East sides and across the Hudson River to New Jersey.

Springsteen establishes the space in the abstract, but the next image is the concrete image of a church door "thrown open." The narrator can "hear the organ's song / But the congregation's gone." The empty church conjures those individuals who have been erased through the destruction of the Towers; however, the vacant space also reminds his global "family" of the difficult emotional process they each must face. Springsteen is addressing not only the complexity of emotions experienced during the grieving process, but also the hardships of grieving collectively when mourners are separated by neighborhoods, city and state lines, national borders, and oceans, as well as by race, creed, and class. Springsteen, his voice breaking, pleads, "Come on, rise up!" not only in a hopeless entreaty for the return of what has been lost, but as an appeal to his global family members to join hands figuratively and mourn together.

Mikhail Bakhtin's notion of "verbal vestments" is especially resonant with regard to the way in which Springsteen incorporates a uniquely Italian American political tradition into this rendering of "My City of Ruins" (88). Springsteen's acoustic performance invokes the solemnity of a eulogy and the overarching structure of white gospel and embraces the idiom of a politically engaged address. His utterances, especially his calling those who died "brothers and sisters," imprinted the nation and the global viewing public as a family in mourning. He did not espouse a rhetoric that called for vengeance or retaliation, but suggested that if people could join "hands" and "rise up"—a refrain that shifts listeners into an active process of grieving—their actions would be bound to "faith" and "love" as well as to an emotional rather than a physical "strength."

As a public figure aware of his complex ethnic identity, when Springsteen engages in these types of oratorical posturings, he is arguably reaching outward so that one's community—whether next-door neighbor or a person living halfway across the globe—is not secondary to one's immediate family but rather an integral part of a larger cultural circle. Italian stereotypical portrayals of *omertà* espoused by popular and iconic texts such as *The Godfather* or *The Sopranos* become displaced by a circle of power that is enlarged through the act of addressing an expansive sense of community and civic responsibility. In Springsteen's or Cuomo's worlds, individuals owe their allegiance to the entire circle, not a small fragment of it. Civic responsibility is constructed around an identity based upon familial interactions and individual connections, but it remains cognizant of all members within the larger community (i.e., nation). In his 1983 inaugural address, Cuomo invoked this immigrant "idea of family mutuality," which includes "the sharing of benefits and burdens fairly for the good of all" when he asked "the family of New York" to engage in a civic responsibility that would unite downstate city dwellers and upstate suburbanites and farmers as well as the wealthy, middle, and working classes (qtd. in Viscusi 238). Almost twenty years later, Springsteen constructed the same rhetorical stance during his performance for the benefit concert; his mourning cry came at an apocalyptic moment. This inclusive call to action dissipated the distance between nearby victim and remote witness. Springsteen invited those who heard "My City of Ruins" to abandon the dispassionate view of spectatorship, and mourn.

Throughout his career, Springsteen's images of working- and middle-class ethnicity, seen through the lens of the Italian American tradition of family bonds and civic responsibility, assist Springsteen in "defin[ing] and impact[ing] the world . . . I can't do it by myself. I need my audience" (qtd. in Levy 52). Springsteen's ability to interact with a larger circle (and create an ever larger circle) contributes to a new strategy for rock and roll musicians to engage with local, regional, and global issues of civic responsibility in ways that are reminiscent of the Irish band U2. Springsteen's connection and adherence to his Italian American civic-minded tradition, in a similar fashion to U2's commitment to the Irish working class, and local and global politics, has elevated him from rock and roll icon of the ethnic (such as Italian Americans or Irish Americans) middle and working classes to a respected civic-minded member of an ethnically diverse global community.

Springsteen, the musician who was named early in his career by Jon Landau as "the future of rock and roll," became the voice for a nation in mourning as a result of his overarching desire "to find an audience that would be a reflection of some imagined community that I had in my head" (qtd. in Dawidoff 30). Springsteen has always been driven to sing the stories of the dispossessed and downtrodden, and later, in the case of September 11, he sings of the murdered and those left behind after their loved ones have been killed. The audacity and grandiosity of the 9/11 attacks in conjunction with the collapse of the Twin Towers brought a heightened sense of vulnerability to those both close to and far away from the attacks' epicenters. In Monmouth County, New Jersey, where Springsteen resides, "nearly 150 people . . . died in the attacks" because they either worked in downtown Manhattan or were firefighters or police (Sawyers 169). "My City of Ruins" became a kind of benediction at many of the funerals and memorial services in New Jersey.

Lawrence Grossberg suggests that "Springsteen empowers his fans, energizes them, within their affective commonality by invoking personal and local images . . . America . . . is always invoked as one's 'hometown'"

(134). What Springsteen did on September 21, 2001, was no different from what he has always done in concert. He felt the pulse of the nation—his "hometown"—and responded in the public sphere by doing his civic duty. America was not merely New York City or his community that evening, nor even the nation as a whole, but part of a global entity. His choices were meant purposefully to bind the nation and the global community together as a family, not only by adapting the song to the circumstance, but also by setting up a performance space that looked more like a church or a temple than a concert hall. Robert Viscusi writes that in *Christ in Concrete,* Pietro Di Donato uses the death of the father Geremio as "the event" that binds the neighborhood together, and Viscusi emphasizes that the Latin root of the word "religion" (*re + ligare*) means a "binding together" (127). Springsteen constructs events in his songs in a similar fashion in order to remind individuals that they are not alone. While this binding of individuals could be examined for its connection to Roman Catholicism (Springsteen was raised Catholic), the Italian American political tradition of family in which Springsteen engages is a pragmatic construction, and his use of Roman Catholic symbols in his songs, especially in "My City of Ruins," augments rather than subsumes his civic-minded purpose.

Much in the same way that Cuomo crafted his keynote address at the 1984 Democratic Convention to "bring people to their senses," Springsteen's rendition of "My City of Ruins" focused on the emotional paralysis that many people lived with after September 11. The narrator's pleading utterance "c'mon rise up" represents the collective horror witnessed while calling for an emotional release in order to move forward. Ironically, two days after Springsteen's performance, Rudolph Giuliani, mayor of New York City at the time, reminded those at a citywide prayer service at Yankee Stadium that St. Paul's Chapel, which was built in 1766, "stood directly in the shadow of the World Trade Center Towers . . . somehow, amid all the destruction and devastation, St. Paul's Chapel still stands—without so much as a broken window." Giuliani's image of the salvaged church seems a far cry from Springsteen's more nuanced evocations. Giuliani remembered those lost that day as "citizens" and "victims"; Springsteen called them "brothers and sisters." Giuliani's politicized rhetoric privileges the chapel almost as a defiant space "amid the ruins of war." Springsteen's "My City of Ruins" attempts to shift the horror from a simplistic battle between good and evil to a poetic appeal to join together in prayer. The refrain focuses on hands praying, pleading, and reaching out for assistance; most important, those "hands" serve as a reminder that life must continue.

Springsteen's phrase "my city of ruins" is also more ethnically inclusive; Giuliani invokes a sense of contentious white privilege in his "the ruins of war" address. Springsteen's choice imbeds Giuliani's reference to the destruction but also suggests that the city has become a ghost

town of the living as well as the dead. Those who have been killed are
not going to return, but those who are alive are not necessarily present
emotionally or mentally. In the midst of the ruins and the empty space
of both "the blood red circle" and the empty church, the loss of lives is
concretized through the images of people who begin to appear in the
narrative. There are "young men on the corner / Like scattered leaves"
and the narrator's loss of his loved one's "sweet kiss," which emphasizes
those who made it out of the Towers or others who watched hopelessly
as the Towers fell. These human figures also remind viewers of the res-
cue workers who labored tirelessly to find survivors, and of those who
waited and still wait for family members to return home. The lyrics "my
brother's / down on his knees" reveal that the narrator is also "ruined"
because his "soul is lost." Springsteen puts aside images of retaliation,
and he refuses to draw a simple binary between "us" and "them." In-
stead, he calls upon "these hands" to pray for "strength," "faith," and
"love." The implicit suggestion within this refrain is that in order to survive a tragedy and not become a "ruined" person—one who cannot see
any other way to gain equilibrium except through a retaliatory act of violence—a human being must reconnect with something larger than the
self. The refrain then pushes against the Italian American *communitas*
while also engaging lyrically and musically with the Negro spiritual tradition. Springsteen suggests that an individual must be grounded in
one's sense of self, which includes one's place within the community. The
refrain calls upon the individual to "rise up," but not without a connection
through a human touch—hands clasped in prayer or clasped in another
person's. This physical connection enables the community to get up off
its "knees." While Springsteen remained a solitary figure during the
broadcast, the chorus arranged in a semicircle behind him joined hands
as they repeated the phrases "rise up" and "with these hands." Springsteen intimates that this touch, both literal and figurative—since he is
separate from the chorus as though in a show of solidarity with those
too numb to reach out—is what makes a community a family.

Springsteen's performance deliberately negated the violent acts of
the terrorists and disavowed the spectacle of the media's repetition of
the Towers' collapse without denying what had transpired. He placed the
loss that many felt—whether they knew someone who had died that day
or not—at the forefront. Springsteen's performance, most especially the
use of repetitions such as "rise up" and "with these hands," can be
viewed as moving the public from shock to an active grieving process.
Springsteen transformed his brand of rock and roll performance to speak
intimately to a grief-stricken nation.

At *Glory Days: A Bruce Springsteen Symposium* held in West Long
Branch, New Jersey in 2005, Springsteen biographer Dave Marsh asserted that Springsteen's albums have always been rough drafts for the
performances that follow each album's release. If a listener, according

to Marsh, did not see Springsteen in concert, he or she could never understand what the music was trying to achieve. Lawrence Grossberg's assessment concurs with Marsh's in that he places the success of Springsteen's music "upon his visual and physical presence" (131). Or, as Peter Gambaccini states, "Springsteen fanatics who couldn't sway their friends on the basis of Boss' [sic] recorded work would always dangle the carrot: 'Wait until you see him in concert'" (89). What these interpretations have in common is the sense that Springsteen's musical success is based partly on the necessity to partake in a communal experience where the audience's response is at least as important as the way in which Springsteen constructs both songs and concerts.

For Springsteen, it is not enough to make an album; he needs to go out on the road to maintain the connection to his "family"—his fans and their community as well as his bandmates. During an appearance on *The Late Show with David Letterman* in 2002 he said, "*Born in the USA*. I think I had half a record and I waited another year, year and a half for like four or five more songs and I didn't like them when I was finished with them so finally I got fed up and we went out anyway." What occurs at a Springsteen concert, then, is not simply the rabble-rousing experience of a gigantic house party gone wild. If that were the case, he would not have introduced *America: A Tribute to Heroes.* Springsteen's energetic stage presence is a carefully orchestrated performance that allows for band synergy and crowd spontaneity and response. Viewers of the *Tribute* were offered a thoughtful and moving alternative way to respond to the shocking event.

Springsteen can be considered not only a recording artist but also a master showman and performance artist as well. He creates purposeful spectacles designed to allow audience members, no matter their backgrounds or ethnic makeup, to shed their domestic worries and empathize with others in exchange for raucous high-volume rock and roll; yet his song lyrics are candid and often brutal examinations of the failures of the American Dream. Springsteen writes narratives about Americans who cannot make ends meet: farm workers, illegal immigrants, unwed mothers who put aside romance for the reality of single-motherhood. He also writes about the dead and those who must survive their loss after the tragedy of September 11. Springsteen's connections to the urban landscape and to his ethnic American roots serve to strengthen his ability to empathize with diverse communities.

A firmly established egalitarian sensibility has always helped Springsteen to transcend the one-size-fits-all label of the commercial music industry. His narrative voice empathizes with his audience's hopes and aspirations while challenging the myth of the American Dream. Unlike the poet Walt Whitman, who, as Greg Smith writes, "envisioned the American working class of the future having a better existence than those of his own day," Springsteen, while he "is strongly concerned with improving the lives of contemporary American workers" is also aware of the limitations of any romantic notions that things will get better (303). Along the way, the connection between audience and performer is made through the use of the humor, irony, joy, rage, and sorrow that are the emotional staples of Springsteen's songs.

Audience members are urged to take an active part alongside Springsteen and the E Street Band through call-and-response techniques. Urban grit and middle-class work ethic, based on his Italian and Irish American Jersey Shore upbringing, are evident in the "improvisation" of laughter and high-testosterone rock and roll that Springsteen regularly delivers. While a Springsteen concert normally allows individuals to feel that they are, for the hours of the concert, not of "'real' space and time . . . Lines of class, politics, and geography . . . seem to dissolve within the 'sacred' space and time of the concert experience" (McCarthy 35–36), the events of September 11th created a "real" moment that could not be easily discarded or dismissed. In that moment, Springsteen had to acknowledge the "real" and forge a bond between community members who were vulnerable and frightened by what had occurred. Springsteen chose to create a more expansive vision of the "ties that bind" a community together in order to dissipate the fear and anger that arose as the shock of the event wore off.

Those who witness a Springsteen concert embrace an ethos that Walker Percy suggests is akin to Kierkegaard's idea of "everydayness," which Percy sees as Springsteen's ability to call upon "how we get lost in our thoughts, lose sight of one another . . . but also, how we find ourselves, through finding one another" (qtd. in Coles 7–8). From the beginning of his career, Springsteen has not only constructed his songs and his performances purposefully to free concertgoers from the working-class ethos that may trap them (even though the songs reflect the categorical trials and tribulations of that experience), but also to remind them that human need and emotions like grief and disappointment are common experiences. June Skinner Sawyers writes, "Springsteen doesn't promise to take away the pain—no one can do that—but he does remind us that we are not alone in our suffering" (170). In Springsteen's world, the only way to survive is by counting on each other—the American Dream may fall apart, but the community stands together. The importance of each individual within the community, no matter his or her status, is what gave Springsteen the agency to reach across class, race, and gender barriers to touch the heart of the nation's shock, grief, and anger after September 11th.

While Springsteen had previously used his public status as a rock and roll celebrity to advocate for a multitude of social-justice causes, he did not turn towards an engaged political discourse until October 1996, when he joined California state representatives in a bid to defeat California's Proposition 209, a proposal designed to reduce affirmative action initiatives within the state. What this suggests is that Springsteen, "[f]or all of the social tensions crackling through his music" (Dawidoff 27–28), preferred his role in civic politics to be enacted through his public persona as a rock and roll performer and not as a speechmaker or politician. Springsteen's reticence to engage directly with politics or politicians can be most clearly seen in his noncommittal response to Ronald Reagan's attempted co-optation of "Born in the USA" during Reagan's reelection bid in the 1984 presidential election. Reagan erroneously interpreted "Born in the USA" as an anthem of conservative politics. The song, far from being the "message of hope" that Reagan believed it to be, points out the ways in which Vietnam veterans had been disenfranchised by the government (qtd. in McCarthy 36). While Springsteen did not confront Reagan publicly, he did suggest that citizens were being manipulated, and that "when Reagan mentioned my name in New Jersey, I felt it was another manipulation, and I had to disassociate myself from the president's kind words" (qtd. in McCarthy 36). Another note must be made of Cuomo's 1984 keynote address at the Democratic National Convention, where he responded directly to Reagan's "city on the hill" metaphor. Cuomo said that the American Dream was only true "for those relative few who are lucky enough to live in its good neighborhoods," as he directly challenged Reagan to go out from the White House to visit other places such as "Appalachia[,] where some people still live in sheds . . . [or] a shelter in Chicago" to meet people who were not prospering or had no opportunity to prosper. While Cuomo used the Italian American political tradition to launch a direct attack on Reagan's ideology, it would be another fifteen years before Springsteen would step out from his role as the working class's troubadour. Once Springsteen made the transformation from rock and roll musician to speechmaker at political rallies, he pushed the boundaries in which he would engage in public discourse about national, state, and local issues. The 2001 benefit concert emerges as a transitory iteration between his public persona of rock and roll icon and presidential stumper, and illuminates his dedication to a larger public discourse with the nation.

Springsteen has written eloquently about the men and women who live through urban decay, agricultural greed, and national tragedy while maintaining a connection to both his hometown and his ethnic roots. Springsteen is "living" what Wole Soyinka claims all writers must: "the paradox that embraces, even interiorizes the barrier, yet insists that the barrier should not be there. . . . [T]his activity takes place on all fronts— it is both elemental and social and political" (222). Springsteen has used the traditions and tropes of Italian American communities not only to enhance his rock and roll persona, but also to address national and global concerns.

Springsteen's performance during *America: A Tribute to Heroes* places the rock and roll block party, which he has been able and happy to provide for the last forty years, offstage, and he makes space for a communal grief that binds individuals not only to the nation but also to the rest of the world. Springsteen's acoustic rendition of "My City of Ruins" became the agent that gave voice to a terrible longing: that what had occurred was a bad dream, that the buildings would be restored, and that loved ones would find their way home. Most important, this iteration served as an encomium that conveyed in its spare refrain the belief that the members of his "family" would one day "rise up" like phoenixes from the ashes of despair and become stronger—individually and collectively— as a consequence of the emotional ties and sense of responsibility for one another that had been forged. Springsteen's work over the past forty years has led him to understand, as Cuomo asserted in 1983, that no one succeeds if anyone fails or is suffering. Springsteen has pushed the boundaries of ethnicity into the public sphere in order to argue for more equitable, humane treatment of "brothers and sisters" around the globe—not merely with those whom one is blood related.

Works Cited

America: A Tribute to Heroes. Dir. Joel Gallen and Beth McCarthy-Miller. Perf. Bruce Springsteen. DVD. Warner Brothers, 2001.

Bakhtin, M.M. "The Problem of Speech Genres." *Speech Genres and Other Late Essays: M.M. Bakhtin.* Ed. Caryl Emerson and Michael Holquist. Austin, TX: U of Texas P, 1986. 60–102.

Coles, Robert. *Bruce Springsteen's America.* New York: Random House, 2003.

Cuomo, Mario. "1984 Democratic National Convention Keynote Address." 16 July 1984. *American Rhetoric.* 2008. 20 February 2010. http://www.american-rhetoric.com/speeches/mariocuomo1984dnc.htm.

Dawidoff, Nicholas. "The Pop Populist." *The New York Times Magazine* 26 Jan. 1997: 27+.

Gambaccini, Peter. *Bruce Springsteen.* New York: Quick Fox, 1979.

Giuliani, Rudolph W. "Mayoral Address." Speech at Citywide Prayer Service. Yankee Stadium, New York. 23 Sept. 2001. *Archives of Rudolph W. Giuliani, 107th Mayor.* 22 Feb. 2010 http://www.nyc.gov/html/records/rwg/html/2001b/prayer_service.html.

Grossberg, Lawrence. "Rockin' with Reagan, or the Mainstreaming of Postmodernity." *Cultural Critique* 10 (1988) 123–49. Print.

Levy, Joe. "Bruce Springsteen: The Rolling Stone Interview." *Rolling Stone* 1 Nov. 2007: 51+.

Marsh, Dave. "Bruce Springsteen and the Creation of Community." *Glory Days: A Bruce Springsteen Symposium.* Sponsored by Penn State U and Monmouth U. Sheraton Eatontown Center, West Long Branch, New Jersey. 9 Sept. 2005.

McCarthy, Kate. "Deliver Me from Nowhere: Bruce Springsteen and the Myth of the American Promised Land." *God in the Details: America Religion in Popular Culture.* Ed. Eric Michael Mazur and Kate McCarthy. NY: Routledge, 2001. 23–45.

Sawyers, June Skinner. *Tougher than the Rest: 100 Best Bruce Springsteen Songs.* New York: Omnibus P, 2006.

Smith, Greg. "Whitman, Springsteen, and the American Working Class." *Midwest Quarterly: A Journal of Contemporary Thought* 41.3 (2000): 302–20.

Springsteen, Bruce. "My City of Ruins." *The Rising.* Columbia Records, 2002.

____. Interview by David Letterman. *The Late Show with David Letterman.* CBS. New York. 2 Aug. 2002. Television.

Tucker, Ken. "Springsteen: The Interview." *Entertainment Weekly* 28 Feb. 2003: 20+.

Viscusi, Robert. *Buried Caesars and Other Secrets of Italian American Writing.* New York: SUNY P, 2006.

Soyinka, Wole. *Art, Dialogue, and Outrage: Essays on Literature and Culture.* New York: Pantheon Books, 1988.

MICHAEL ANTONUCCI

AFTERWORD: FOUNDING DISCUSSIONS
Building Sophistications

The consequences of my decision to accept an invitation to serve as re-spondent at a Modern Language Association's Discussion Group on Ital-ian American literature forum held at the 2007 MLA convention in Chicago have been profound and humbling. Predictably, saying "yes" was the easy part. Upon learning to whom I would be responding, my sense of ease quickly changed. Mary Jo Bona, Teresa Fiore, Fred L. Gardaphè, Edvige Giunta, Josphine Gattuso Hendin, and Anthony Julian Tamburri: seeing the roster of names made me begin to question what sort of "response" I was qualified to deliver after they'd had their say. As writers and schol-ars—or both—these people had shaped and defined Italian American lit-erary studies, established the Discussion Group and taken the field—to paraphrase Anthony Tamburri—far beyond "nonna and pizza."

Even under so-called ordinary circumstances, a meeting of the American Italian Historical Association (AIHA) or Multiethnic Literature of the United States (MELUS), for instance, responding directly to a gath-ering of prominent scholars would have carried its own degree of diffi-culty. I had been introduced to Professors Bona, Gardaphè, and Tamburri through these organizations and came to know them as supportive and skilled listeners, dedicated to cultivating and developing an emerging generation of scholars in the field of Italian/American literary and cultural studies. And while the assignment of offering a direct response to these pathfinders and ground breakers would have been daunting within the context of these institutional settings, it was of course compounded by the idea that this would take place at the Modern Language Assoiciation's Annual Convention in Chicago, the hometown of Professors Gardaphè and Bona. My sense of this became especially evident when I learned the title for the forum: "Perspectives on the Future of the Italian Amer-ican Literature Discussion Group: Ten Years Later."

Under these circumstances, the prospect of working with this senior set of Italian American literary scholars became as intimidating as it was exhilarating. I decided that the best approach to delivering a response would come by way of summary. My contribution to the proceedings, therefore, would be gathering a sense of what Professors Bona, Fiore, Gardaphè, Giunta, Hendin and Tamburri were suggesting about a decade's worth of work in Italian American literary studies. This thought provided me great comfort, allowing me to find a way of joining the voices of those whose efforts had actually made the event possible.

After settling on an approach underwritten, perhaps in large part, by the proverb "*La migliore parola è quella che non si dice,*"[1] I undertook a review of the work that these scholars had produced as they established the MLA Discussion Group on Italian American literature. Retracing their steps, contextualizing their efforts and their vision provided me with a deep sense of appreciation and respect for their individual contributions to a shared project: each book, each article, each conference presentation contributed to a larger project, rooted in the goal of expanding and developing a field of study. I can report that by pursuing a "response-through-summary" strategy, my comments at the forum focused on what those present at the founding of the Discussion Group had to say as they recalled and assessed ten years of hard work. Returning to write about Italian American literary studies at the outset of the Discussion Group's second decade of existence, my response is shaped and directed by the experience of being present on that December night in Chicago.

As this volume's table of contents indicates, growth and development in the field of Italian American literary studies continues, encompassing a variety of interests and areas of inquiry. Accessing a range of issues that include image and identity, gender, the color line, poetics, space, place, and geography, the critical activity of Italian American literary studies seems to be approaching a level of "sophistication" that Fred Gardaphè imagined while he was a graduate student reading Henry Louis Gates Jr.'s "Criticism in the Jungle." With his essay "Breaking and Entering," Gardaphè recalls the influence that Gate's essay had on his development as a scholar and institution builder, considering its use of Du Bois and how it delivers the axiom, "All great writers demand great critics." In this way, with his contribution to A. Kenneth Ciongoli and Jay Parini's *Beyond the Godfather* (1997), Gardaphè effectively underscores the institutional and intellectual necessity for establishing organizations dedicated to cultivating the critical study of Italian American literature and culture. Not surprisingly, the appeal that Gardaphè makes in "Breaking

---

[1] Mary Jo Bona uses and translates this phrase as "the best word is that which is not spoken" in the introduction of her study *Claiming a Tradition: Italian American Women Writers* (14).

and Entering" appeared in Ciongoli and Parini's volume at the same time that the MLA would have been considering the proposal to create a new Discussion Group on Italian American literature.

As the Discussion Group enters its second decade, it would appear that the institution-building efforts and scholarly production of the 1990s have succeeded. Evidence of the critical "sophistication" that Gardaphè recognized as a significant component with respect to Italian American literary studies growth is present in the arrival of a "next wave" of Italian American literary studies. Not only have the continuities and conversations that have emerged from these initiatives become evident among critics and writers, but they have also extended themselves across perspectives and generations. We see an example of this dynamic when we read Mary Jo Bona's *Claiming a Tradition: Italian American Women Writers* (1999), which concludes with a chapter entitled "Recent Developments in Italian American Women's Literary Traditions." In this portion of the study Bona examines Carole Maso's *Ghost Dance* and Rachel Guido DeVries's *Tender Warriors.* Understanding that with their novels Maso and DeVries make important contributions to an extended conversation about Italian American family and gender relations, Bona claims that their work seeks to "honor and challenge those traditions of *italianità* integral to their identities as woman and as writers" (197). She presents the protagonist of Maso's novel, Vanessa Turin, and DeVries's Rose De-Marco character to illustrate her claim that "ethnicity is a governing identity and as such must be reinterpreted by every generation" (188).

A full decade after making this claim, Bona's observation is underscored as JoAnne Ruvoli-Gruba and Michele Fazio explore *Ghost Dance* and *Tender Warriors* by bringing Maso's work into direct conversation with the challenges posed by DeVries in her novel. Importantly, Ruvoli-Gruba and DeFazio advance distinct readings of the interplay between Maso and DeVries's fiction with essays that are included in Paolo A. Giordano and Anthony Julian Tamburri's *Italian Americans in the Third Millennium* (2009).

While both of these emerging scholars draw upon Bona's pioneering work, their essays develop interpretations of *Ghost Dance* and *Tender Warriors* that extend and expand this conversation. In "The Absence of Memory: Unreliable Storytelling in *Tender Warriors* and *Ghost Dance*," Ruvoli-Gruba explores Maso's and DeVries's use of narrating characters in their novels to "question dominant power structures such as the traditionally ethnic patriarchal family, a capitalist economy, and systems of culture and history" (161). Fazio's "Locating Mother: Performing Italian American and Native American Rituals in *Tender Warriors* and *Ghost Dance*" focuses on "ritualistic performances" carried out by the protagonists of these novels. According to Fazio, Maso and DeVries:

. . . encourage their readers to consider the future of Italian American family, and by doing so make evident that as sons and daughters, [we] have the creative power to heal ourselves and to end destructive patterns that divide us from one another. (87)

As they work toward their own ends, Ruvoli-Gruba and Fazio both read Maso and DeVries with respect to literary and cultural traditions other than those rooted in Italian American experience. Fazio brings critical attention to the way that characters in *Ghost Dance* and *Tender Warriors* engage with figures outside of the Italian American community. Her essay examines interactions between DeVries's Sonny DeMarco and figures that represent members of various subaltern groups he encounters at the Quick Star Diner. Similarly, she also explores Maso's use of Plains Indian healing practices and survival strategies by Vanessa and Fletcher in *Ghost Dance.* Fazio complicates the discussion of Italian American ethnicity, as it is delivered in these novels through her use of an anthropological lens. Similarly, Ruvoli-Gruba's essay understands Maso and DeVries as working within the "the tradition of feminist experimental writing" (164). By doing so, she effectively creates an intersectional reading of these novels, inviting consideration of them both as literary works by Italian American female writers and within conversations about experimental writing writ large. In this way, Ruvoli-Gruba joins Fazio in complicating received notions about the limits and capacities of Italian American literature.

The strong and varied readings that the Maso and DeVries novels receive from Bona, Ruvoli-Gruba, and Fazio ultimately direct attention from critical and theoretical discussions of Italian American literary work to the production of Italian/American literature itself. As the focus shifts, questions arise: Who is writing the kind of compelling Italian American literature that attracts the attention of these scholars? Does contemporary Italian American literature enter critical engagements with and evaluations of Italian American identity within and beyond the limits of the Italian/American culture, including family and community? Where does recent Italian American literary work exhibit an impulse toward formal experimentation while exploring complex, even painful, aspects of Italian/American experience? In what ways do these works contribute to a project of advancing "the critical sophistication" within Italian American literary studies?

As the MLA Discussion Group on Italian American literature enters its second decade, scholars, critics and writers interested in grappling with these questions are in a good position. Challenging and engaging literary works by Italian American writers is plentiful, including the poetry of Jennifer Scappettone and Peter Covino as well as fiction by Dana Spiotta. Poetry by Raymond L. Bianchi also provides an entry point for those who would respond to these queries. With verse that maintains a particular sense of the diasporic, transcontinental dimensions of *italianità,* this

Chicago-based poet works along the hard edges of landscapes shaped by forces unleashed in a relentless, unyielding modernity. Through his poetry Bianchi plumbs depths where politics, ethics, faith, and inheritance intersect.

Bianchi engages these themes in his volume *Immediate Empire* (2008). His verse probes, questions, identifies, provokes, and awakens, effectively staging a poetic pageant that passes through territories marked "AMERICA." As *Immediate Empire* negotiates various narrow passages—church, state, Chicago, dogmas, heresies, consumption, TV, the frontier, fascism—it effectively enacts its own open door policy (breaking and entering) from Tierra del Fuego to Stone Park, via the Chicago Sanitary and Ship Canal. It is sophisticated, demanding literary work. As such, it delivers the kind of work that the founders of MLA Discussion Group on Italian American literature might have imagined as contributing to a broad and ranging conversation concerned with literary production by Italian Americans.

Works Cited

Bianchi, Ramond. *Immediate Empire.* Los Angeles: i.e Press, 2008.

Bona, Mary Jo. *Claiming Tradition: Italian American Women Writers.* Carbondale, IL: Southern Illinois UP, 1999.

Fazio, Michele. "Locating Mother: Performing Italian American and Native American Rituals in *Tender Warriors* and *Ghost Dance.*" Giordano and Tamburri 75–87.

Gardaphè, Fred. "Breaking and Entering." *Beyond The Godfather: Italian American Writers on the Real Italian American Experience.* Ed. A. Kenneth Ciongoli and Jay Parini. Hanover, NH: UP of New England, 1997.

Giordano, Paolo A., and Anthony Julian Tamburri, eds. *Italian Americans in the Third Millennium.* New York: American Italian Historical Association, 2009.

Ruvoli-Gruba, JoAnne. "The Absence of Memory: Unreliable Story Telling in *Tender Warriors* and *Ghost Dance.*" Giordano and Tamburri 160–76.

Appendix

Discussion Group on Italian American Literature
Executive Committee Members, 1998–2010

Mary Jo Bona
Josephine Gattuso Hendin
Anthony Julian Tamburri
Fred Gardaphe
Edvige Giunta
George Guida
John Domini
Tracy Floreani
Maria S. Trubiano
Michele Fazio
Dennis Barone
Peter Covino
JoAnne Ruvoli
Michael Antonucci
Tom Cerasulo
Jim Cocola

* * *

Discussion Group on Italian American Literature
MLA Convention Programs, 1998–2010

San Francisco, 1998
"Staking Claims: Defining Italian American Cultural Studies"
Presiding: Mary Jo Bona
Italian American Insights and the Nineties, Josephine Gattuso Hendin
Origins: The Evolution of Italian American Narratives, Fred Gardaphe
Into the Twenty-First Century: The Future of Italian American Narratives,
    Anthony Julian Tamburri
Respondent: Edvige Giunta

Chicago, 1999
"Saint and Sinners: Shaping an Italian American Canon"
Presiding: Josephine Gattuso Hendin
Canon and Identity in the Italian American Cinema, Aaron B. Baker and
Juliann M. Vitullo
Toward an Italo-American Sublime in The Godfather, Alessia Ricciardi
*"Like a Dancing Bear": The Sopranos Brings the Media to the Mafia and
Class Unease to Italian America,* John Domini
Respondent: Mary Jo Bona

Washington, DC, 2000
"Ma(Donna): The Image of Italian American Women in Literature, Film
and Television"
Presiding: Anthony Julian Tamburri
*Rescuing the Fallen Woman: The Issue of Female Representation in Mar-
tin Scorsese's Cinema,* Dorothe M. Bonnigal
Anything but Italian: Madonna's Synthetic Ethnicity, William Van Watson
Italian American Women as Comic Foils: Exploding the Stereotype in My
Cousin Vinny, Moonstruck, *and* Married to the Mob, Mary Ann McDon-
ald Carolan
Transgressive Italian American Women in Carole Maso's Ghost Dance,
Nancy Savoca's Household Saints, *and David Chase's* The Sopranos,
Mary Jo Bona

New Orleans, 2001
"Lynchings and Linkings: Italian Americans in Hybrid America"
Presiding: Fred Gardaphe
Ethnicity Gone Wild: An Ecological Lineage in Italian American Poetry,
Anthony Francis Lioi
The Very Strange Truth: Ben Piazza's Italian Southerner, Tracy Floreani
*Where Are the Italian Anarchists? Amiri Baraka and the Pluralist Politics
of Dissent,* Matthew Calihan
A Man Called Cody: Race and the Passing of a Sicilian in New Orleans,
Joseph Conte

New York, 2002
"Assimilate This! Migration, Metropolis, and 'mericans in Italian Ameri-
can Culture"
Presiding: Edvige Giunta
City Moves, Kathleen McCormick
Anger and Assimilation in New York: Louis Forgione's The River Between
(1928), Dennis Barone
*Memory, Knowledge, and Testimonial Writing: Italian American and Ital-
ian Women's Memoirs,* Serena Anderlini-D'Onofrio
*Shrinking Italians: The Travails of Psychoanalysis and American Assim-
ilation,* Stefania Lucamante

San Diego, 2003
"Westward, O! Italian American Cultural Trajectories"
Presiding: George Guida
Rome If You Want To: The Currency of John Fante's Italy, Dennis Barone
Going Native: Italian Americans as Indians in Carole Maso's Ghost Dance,
    Michele Fazio
Westward Soprano: Route to Roots? Examining the Italian American Ethnic Identity Percorso of Tony Soprano in HBO's The Sopranos, Paul
    A. Galante

Philadelphia, 2004
"The Poetry of Resistance: When Wal-Mart Comes to Little Italy"
Presiding: John Domini
The Black Hand Becomes the Big Box: Two Poets of South Philadelphia,
    Dennis Barone
Sausage and Peppers Aren't on the Menu: Bob Giraldi's Dinner Rush,
    Paul A. Galante

Washington, DC, 2005
"Translated Lives: Negotiations of Self in Italian America"
Presiding: Tracy Floreani
Translating Voices in Mary di Michele's Tenor of Love, Ian Williams
"Sometimes Spaghetti Likes to Be Alone": Food as Medium for Translating the Complexities of Italian American Identity, Rita M. Colanzi
Ralph Fasanella's Visual Narrative and Epic Visions, Janet Zandy

Philadelphia, 2006
"Juxtapositions: Teaching Italian American Literature"
Presiding: Marissa S. Trubiano
Bringing Stories to Ethnic History: Pedagogical Strategies for Teaching Italian American Literature in the Millennium, Mary Jo Bona
Hyphenated Hybridizations: Teaching Italian American Literature, Rose
    De Angelis
Modern Agoras: A Comparitivist Study of Public Teaching at Italian American Institutes, Gina Miele

Chicago, 2007
"Perspectives on the Future of the Italian American Literature Discussion
    Group: Ten Years Later"
Presiding: Michele Fazio
Speakers: Mary Jo Bona, Teresa Fiore, Fred Gardaphe, Josephine Gattuso
    Hendin
Respondent: Michael A. Antonucci

San Francisco, 2008
"Italian American Literary Innovation"

Presiding: Dennis Barone

Sick of Brick: The Critical Reception of di Donato's Later Novels, Tom Cerasulo

From Change to Follies: The Progressive Subversions of Gilbert Sorrentino and Why They Work, John Domini

"Upsetting the Lexical Surfaces": Language, Revolution, and Italian American Identity in the Cross-Genre Writing of Carole Maso, Roseanne Giannini Quinn

Philadelphia, 2009

"Exploring Italian American Poetry: History, Key Figure(s), Trends, Related Issues"

Presiding: Peter Covino

Mother's Tongue: Italian American Poets and Literary Revisionism, Mary Jo Bona

"Upsettin da Setuppa": Vincent Ferrini's Dialect Poetry, Jim Cocola

Antonello Borra's Bestiary: An Italian and American Updating, Blossom S. Kirschenbaum

Due to changing the annual MLA Convention from late December to early January, there was no 2010 meeting.

Contributors

MICHAEL A. ANTONUCCI'S scholarly work is available or will soon appear in *African American Review, American Studies Journal, Brilliant Corners, Callaloo, Cold Mountain Review, Valley Voices,* and *Rain Taxi.* His creative work, including collaborative writing produced as a member of the Jimmy Wynn Ensemble, has appeared in *Admit 2, The Cortland Review, Exquisite Corpse,* and *Seven Corners.* He is Assistant Professor in the American Studies Program and English Department at Keene State College and currently co-editing *Chance Commands,* a volume of critical and creative work in conversation with the poetry of Sterling D. Plumpp.

DENNIS BARONE is the author of *America / Trattabili,* a study of Italian American narrative published by Bordighera Press in 2011 and editor of *New Hungers for Old: One-Hundred Years of Italian American Poetry* (Star Cloud Press, 2011). He is also the author of several books of fiction and poetry. He is Director of American Studies at Saint Joseph College in West Hartford, Connecticut.

NANCY CARONIA, a PhD candidate and Teaching Assistant in the University of Rhode Island English Department, has been a Springsteen fan for many years. She is currently at work on *Personal Effects: Essays on Memory, Culture, and Women in the Work of Louise DeSalvo,* with co-editor Edvige Giunta. She received an MA from SUNY Brockport where she was awarded the English Department's Blaine DeLancey Memorial Award for her critical scholarship on Walt Whitman and Bharati Mukherjee and the Calvin Rich Poetry Award for her poetry.

JIM COCOLA is an Assistant Professor of Literature, Film, and Media in the Department of Humanities and Arts at Worcester Polytechnic Institute, and also serves on the faculty of the Language and Thinking Program at Bard College. He received his AB from the Committee on Degrees in History and Literature at Harvard College and his PhD from the Department of English at the University of Virginia, completing his dissertation under the auspices of the Georgia O'Keeffe Museum Research Center in Santa Fe, New Mexico. He has published essays and reviews in *Discourse,* the *minnesota review, n+1,* and *SEL: Studies in English Literature 1500–1900.*

JOSEPH CONTE is Professor of English at the University at Buffalo. His book, *Debris & Design: A Chaotics of Postmodern American Fiction,* received the Elizabeth Agee Prize from the University of Alabama Press in 2002. He was a Senior Fellow at the New York Institute of Cognitive and Cultural Studies in St. Petersburg, Russia in 2005. In 2009 he was a Visiting Professor of English at Capital Normal University in Beijing, China. He has published essays on Don DeLillo in *The Cambridge Companion to Don DeLillo,* on Gilbert Sorrentino in *Critique,* and on *The Sopranos* in *The Buffalo News.*

Poet, translator, and essayist **PETER COVINO** is the author the poetry collections, both from New Issues – W. Michigan UP, *The Right Place to Jump* (2012) and *Cut Off the Ears of Winter,* winner of the 2007 PEN American/Osterweil Award. Recent poems and essays have appeared in the *American Poetry Review, Colorado Review, Modern Language Association* (text book series), *The Paris Review,* and *The Yale Review,* among other journals. He is an Assistant Professor of English at the University of Rhode Island, and poetry editor for *VIA: Voices in Italian Americana.*

JOHN DOMINI has published two books of stories, the latest *Highway Trade* (1998), and three novels, the latest *A Tomb on the Periphery* (2008). His 2007 novel *Earthquake I.D.,* in Italian translation, was the runner-up for the 2009 Domenica Rea award. His criticism has appeared in *The New York Times, The Believer,* and elsewhere, and he has often presented at the Modern Languages Association Annual Convention. He has held Visiting Writer appointments at Northwestern, Harvard, and elsewhere.

TRACY FLOREANI is Associate Professor of English at Oklahoma City University, where she serves as department chair and teaches courses in American and contemporary multiethnic literature. Her recent work also includes the development of interdisciplinary initiatives in the teaching of social justice. Her scholarship focuses primarily on novelistic and mass media representations of ethnic minorities and immigrants to the U.S. at the middle of the twentieth century.

KATHLEEN ZAMBONI MCCORMICK is Professor of Literature at SUNY Purchase. Much of her scholarship focuses on developing new teaching practices, particularly in the areas of student writing and research, as can be seen in *Reading Our Histories, Understanding Our Culture,* in over 50 articles on the subject, and in *The Culture of Reading and the Teaching of English,* which won the MLA's Mina Shaughnessy Award. Recently, she has begun work in Italian American studies and is the co-editor of the MLA volume

Teaching Italian American Literature and is finishing a memoir, *Why is God in Daddy's Slippers?* on growing up as a half-Italian/half-Irish-American. Chapters have appeared in *Witness, South Carolina Review, Rambler, Italian Americana,* among others.

GINA M. MIELE is Assistant Professor of Italian and former Director of the Coccia Institute for the Italian Experience in America at Montclair State University in New Jersey. She has published articles on the folktales of Luigi Capuana and Italo Calvino in *Italica, Marvels and Tales, Fabula,* and *Italian Quarterly.* She is a contributor to the *Greenwood Encyclopedia of Folktales and Fairy Tales.* Her essays and book reviews on Italian American studies can be consulted in the *Harvard College Journal of Italian American History and Culture,* the *Italian American Review,* the *Paterson Literary Review,* and *Primo.*

ROSEANNE GIANNINI QUINN is Associate Professor of English, and also teaches women's studies, at De Anza College in the San Francisco Bay area. Her research interests center on Italian American women's multi-genre writing, multi-ethnic feminist theory, and contemporary popular culture. Her most recent publication is included in the MLA anthology entitled *Teaching Italian American Literature, Film, and Popular Culture,* edited by Edvige Giunta and Kathleen Zamboni McCormick.

INDEX

SAGGISTICA

Taking its name from the Italian — which means essays, essay writing, or non fiction —
Saggisitca *is a referred book series dedicated to the study of all topics, individuals, and cultural productions that fall under what we might consider that larger umbrella of all things Italian and Italian/American.*

Vito Zagarrio
> The "Un-Happy Ending": *Re-viewing The Cinema of Frank Capra.* 2011.
> ISBN 978-1-59954-005-4. Volume 1.

Paolo A. Giordano, editor
> *The Hyphenate Writer and The Legacy of Exile.* 2010.
> ISBN 978-1-59954-007-8. Volume 2.

Dennis Barone
> *America / Trattabili.* 2011. ISBN 978-1-59954-018-4. Volume 3.

Fred L. Gardaphè
> *The Art of Reading Italian Americana.* 2011. ISBN 978-1-59954-019-1. Volume 4.

Anthony Julian Tamburri
> *Re-viewing Italian Americana: Generalities and Specificities on Cinema.* 2011.
> ISBN 978-1-59954-020-7. Volume 5.

Sheryl Lynn Postman
> *An Italian Writer's Journey through American Realities: Giose Rimanelli's English Novels. "The most tormented decade of America: The 60s."*
> ISBN 978-1-59954-034-4. Volume 6.

Luigi Fontanella
> *Migrating Words: Italian Writers in the United States.*
> ISBN 978-1-59954-041-2. Volume 7.

The following volume is forthcoming:
Peter Carravetta
> *After Identity: Critical Challenges in Italian American Poetics and Culture.*
> ISBN 978-1-59954-036-8. Volume 9.

www.ingramcontent.com/pod-product-compliance
Lightning Source LLC
LaVergne TN
LVHW091314080426
835510LV00007B/493